The Apostles' Creed

ROBERT M. HADDAD

Nihil Obstat: Rev. Peter Joseph, STD.

Imprimatur: + Julian Porteous, DD, VG,

Date: 13th November, 2003

The Nihil Obstat and Imprimatur are a declaration that a book or pamphlet is considered to be free from doctrinal or moral error. It is not necessarily implied that those who have granted them agree with the contents, opinions or statements expressed.

Scripture quotes taken from the **Revised Standard Version of the Bible (Second Catholic Edition)**, copyright © 2006 (Ignatius Press).

Extracts from **The Faith of the Early Fathers,** Rev. William A. Jurgens, copyright © 1970 by The Order of St. Benedict, Inc., The Liturgical Press, Collegeville, Minnesota. Used with permission.

Extracts from **The Roman Catechism**, Issued by order of Pope St. Pius V, 1566, reprinted by TAN Books and Publishers Inc., Rockford, Illinois 61105.

Extracts from English translation of **Catechism of the Catholic Church** for Australia copyright © June 1994 St. Pauls/Libreria Editrice Vaticana. Used with permission.

Cover design: Parousia Media, PO Box 59, Galston, NSW, 2159.
www.parousiamedia.com

Published by: Parousia Media.

© Robert M. Haddad 2014. All rights reserved. Extracts and copies of various parts or chapters of the series may be made in cases of 'fair dealing', viz., for the purpose of teaching, promoting and defending the Catholic Faith. All acknowledgments given to Robert M. Haddad.

ISBN: 978-1-922660-61-9

Contents

Foreword	v
Introduction	1
I Believe in God, the Father Almighty	5
Creator of Heaven and Earth	11
Creator of Heaven and Earth: Angels	16
Creator of Heaven and Earth: Man	21
And in Jesus Christ, His Only Son, Our Lord	25
Who was Conceived by the Holy Spirit Born of the Virgin Mary	30
Suffered Under Pontius Pilate, was Crucified, Died and was Buried	35
He Descended into Hell, the Third Day He Rose Again from the Dead	40
He Ascended into Heaven; is Seated at the Right Hand of God the Father Almighty	44
From Thence He Shall Come to Judge the Living and the Dead	48
I Believe in the Holy Spirit	53
The Holy Catholic Church	59
The Communion of Saints	66
The Forgiveness of Sins	72
The Resurrection of the Body	77
And Life Everlasting. Amen.	83
Appendix: Creeds through the Ages	88
About the Author	111
Other Works by the Author	112

Foreword

If man knew his religion ...

"Neither wealth, nor honors, nor vanity can make a man happy during his life on earth, but only attachment to the service of God, when we are fortunate enough to realize that and to carry it out properly. The woman who is held in contempt by her husband is not unhappy in her state because she is held in contempt but because she does not know her religion or because she does not practise what her religion tells her she should do. Teach her her religion, and from the moment that you see her practise it, she will cease to complain and to consider herself unhappy. Oh! How happy man would be, even on this earth, if he knew his religion!

What power that person who is near to God possesses when he loves Him and serves Him faithfully! Alas, my dear brethren, anyone who is despised by worldly people, who appears to be unimportant and humble, look at him when he masters the very will and power of God Himself. Look at Moses, who compels the Lord to grant pardon to three hundred thousand men who were indeed guilty. Look at Josue, who commanded the sun to stand still and the sun became immobile, a thing which never happened before and which perhaps will never happen again. Look at the Apostles: simply because they loved God, the devils fled before them, the lame walked, the blind saw, the dead arose to life. Look at St Benedict, who commanded the rocks to stop in their course and they remained hanging in mid-air. Look at him who multiplied bread, who made water come out of the rocks, and who disposed of the stones and the forest as easily as if they were wisps of straw. Look at St Francis of Paula who commands the fish to come to hear the word of God and they respond to his call with such loyalty that they applaud his words. Look at St John who commands the birds to keep silent and they obey him. Look at many others who walk the seas without any human aid. Very well! Now take a look at all those impious people and all those famous ones of the world with all their wit and all their knowledge for achieving everything. Alas! Of what are they really capable? Of nothing at all. And why not? Unless it is because they are not attached to the service of God. But how powerful and how happy at the same time is the person who knows his religion and who practises what it commands ..."

Sermons of St John Vianney,
for the Fourteenth Sunday after Pentecost.

Introduction

"For man believes with his heart and so is justified, and he confesses with his lips and so is saved" (Rom. 10:10).

The word "creed" is derived from the Latin *"credo"*, meaning "I believe." A creed as understood traditionally by the Church is a body of beliefs set down in precise form to be held by all the faithful.

Creeds have been a means of expressing the Catholic Faith since earliest times. Having received her commission from Our Lord Jesus Christ to preach the Gospel to "the whole creation" (Mk 16:15), the Church in time thought it prudent that the principal articles of belief be reduced to brief formulae which could be recited and memorized by all. Each formula became known as a *Symbolum*, or sign. Through such means, all the faithful would be "united in the same mind and the same judgment" (1 Cor. 1:10), thwarting division and schism.

As the visible Mystical Body of Christ, the Church and its members are called upon not only to hold the same beliefs but to express those same beliefs publicly: "For man believes with his heart and so is justified, and he confesses with his lips and so is saved" (Rom. 10:10). This confession is to be of "sound words which you have heard from me, in the faith and love which are in Christ Jesus" (2 Tim. 1:13). Hence, the requirement that catechumens recite the Creed before they are baptized and the baptized before they are confirmed.

The principal Creeds of the Catholic Church are the *Apostles'*, *Athanasian*, *Nicene*, *Pius IV's* and the *Credo of the People of God*. There exist also various special formulas drawn up according to the circumstances of time and place to have the Church's teaching expressly stated and accepted, for example, those prescribed by Pope Innocent III for the Waldensians, and Pope Gregory XIII for the Greeks. Of all these, the Apostles' Creed is regarded by scholars as the most ancient, being traceable in its various parts to the second century AD.

These twelve articles can be divided into three groups: the first, those referring to God the Father and His work of creation; the second, those referring to Jesus Christ and His work of redemption; the third, those referring to the Holy Spirit and His work of sanctification. It is this

Apostles' Creed which this book will expound article by article.

When a Catholic recites the Apostles' Creed he does not merely express his own personal beliefs but is affirming eternal truths revealed to the Church by God Himself. Those who reject Creeds as a means of expressing the Christian Faith usually do so because they have abandoned belief in the ancient articles contained within them, often replacing them with personal opinions no more ancient than themselves. Nevertheless, some Protestants over the centuries have formulated a number of their own creeds, namely, the "Augsburg Confession", the "Confession of Basle", the "Thirty-Nine Articles", etc.; however, these are in substance no more than a collection of the private views, opinions or theories of their original founders, often incorporating articles which are specifically anti-Catholic.

The Fathers

St Irenaeus of Lyons, *Against Heresies* 1, 10, 1 (c. AD 180)

"For the Church, although dispersed throughout the whole world even to the ends of the earth, has received from the Apostles and from their disciples the faith in one God, Father Almighty, the Creator of heaven and earth and sea and all that is in them; and in one Jesus Christ, the Son of God who became flesh for our salvation; and in the Holy Spirit, who announced through the prophets the dispensations and the comings; and the birth from a Virgin, and the passion, and the resurrection from the dead, and the bodily ascension into heaven in the glory of the Father to re-establish all things; and the raising up again of all flesh of all humanity, in order that to Jesus Christ our Lord and God and Savior and King, in accord with the approval of the invisible Father, every knee shall bend of those in heaven and on earth and under the earth, and that every tongue shall confess Him, and that He may make just judgment of them all; and that He may send the spiritual forces of wickedness and the angels who transgressed and became apostates, and the impious, unjust, lawless and blasphemous amongst men, into everlasting fire; and that He may grant life, immortality, and surround with eternal glory the just and the holy."

Introduction

Tertullian, *Against Praxeas* 2, 1 (post AD 213)
"We do indeed believe that there is only one God; but we believe that under this dispensation ... there is also a Son of this one only God, His Word, who proceeded from Him and through whom all things were made and without whom nothing was made. We believe that He was sent by the Father into a Virgin and was born of her, God and man, Son of man and Son of God, and was called by the name Jesus Christ. We believe that He suffered and that, in accord with the Scriptures, He died and was buried; and that He was raised again by the Father to resume His place in heaven, sitting at the right of the Father; and that He will come to judge the living and the dead. We believe that He sent down from the Father, in accord with His own promise, the Holy Spirit, the Paraclete, the Sanctifier of the faith of those who believe in the Father and in the Son and in the Holy Spirit ... That this rule of faith has been current since the beginning of the Gospel, before even the earlier heretics."

St Hippolytus of Rome, *The Apostolic Tradition* 21 (c. AD 215-217)
"Do you believe in God, the Father almighty? Do you believe in Jesus Christ, the Son of God, who was born of the Virgin Mary by the Holy Spirit, has been crucified under Pontius Pilate, died [and was buried], who, on the third day rose again, alive, from the dead, ascended into heaven and took His seat at the right hand of the Father, and shall come to judge the living and the dead? Do you believe in the Holy Church and the resurrection of the body in the Holy Spirit?"

St Cyril of Jerusalem, *Catechetical Lectures* 5, 12 (c. AD 350)
"This synthesis of faith was not made to accord with human opinions, but rather what was of the greatest importance was gathered from all the Scriptures, to present the one teaching of the faith in its entirety. And just as the mustard seed contains a great number of branches in a tiny grain, so too this summary of faith encompassed in a few words the whole knowledge of the true religion contained in the Old and New Testaments."

St Ambrose of Milan, *Exposition on the Faith* 1 (c. AD 379)
"This Creed is the spiritual seal, our hearts' meditation and an ever-present guardian; it is, unquestionably, the treasure of our soul."

The Roman Catechism (1566)

Preface: Now the chief truths which Christians ought to hold are those which the holy Apostles, the leaders and teachers of the faith, inspired by the Holy Ghost, have divided into the twelve Articles of the Creed. For having received a command from the Lord to go forth *into the whole world*, as His ambassadors, *and preach the Gospel to every creature*, they thought it advisable to draw up a formula of Christian faith, that all might think and *speak the same thing*, and that among those whom they should have called to the unity of the faith no schisms would exist, but that they should be *perfect in the same mind, and in the same judgment*.

Catechism of the Catholic Church (1992)

No. 186: From the beginning, the apostolic Church expressed and handed on her faith in brief formulae for all. But already early on, the Church also wanted to gather the essential elements of its faith into organic and articulated summaries, intended especially for candidates for Baptism.

No. 187: Such syntheses are called "professions of faith" since they summarize the faith that Christians profess. They are called "creeds" on account of what is usually their first word in Latin: *credo* ("I believe"). They are also called "symbols of faith."

No. 194: *The Apostles' Creed* is so called because it is rightly considered to be a faithful summary of the apostles' faith. It is the ancient baptismal symbol of the Church of Rome. Its great authority arises from this fact: it is "the Creed of the Roman Church, the See of Peter, the first of the apostles, to which he brought the common faith."

I Believe in God, the Father Almighty

"The fool says in his heart, 'There is no God'" (Ps. 14:1).

In the first article of the Creed we state our belief in one infinite, self-existent Being, a supreme Spirit possessing every perfection in an infinite degree, having no beginning and no end.

Being infinite, God possesses infinite power (omnipotence), knows all things (omniscience), and is present everywhere (omnipresence). Moreover, God is infinitely wise, holy, just, merciful, true and faithful. Outside of Himself all created things depend on God for their existence. God's providence takes an account of all the works of His hands and all our thoughts, words and works: "but it is thy providence, O Father, that steers its course, because thou hast given it a path in the sea, and a safe way through the waves" (Wis. 14:3).

God is one and unchangeable, single in nature: "Hear, O Israel: The Lord our God is one Lord" (Deut. 6:4). Yet in this *one divine nature* there are *three Persons*, the Father, the Son, and the Holy Spirit. Despite being numerically distinct from each other these three Persons have one and the same indivisible divine nature and substance. The Father, the Son, and the Holy Spirit are all truly God – yet these three Persons are not three separate Gods, but one God in *Trinity*. As Persons they are distinct, in substance they are one: "There are three that give testimony in heaven, the Father, the Word, and the Holy Spirit: and these three are one" (1 Jn 5:7).[1]

In the language of Scripture, certain qualities are attributed to each Divine Person pre-eminently: power and creation are attributed to the Father; wisdom and redemption to the Son; holiness and

---

[1] Douai Version. Since the pronouncement of the Biblical Commission in 1927, it is open to Biblical exegetes to question the Scriptural authenticity of this verse. This stems from the fact that it is not found in any of the extant ancient Greek manuscripts, but only in later Latin versions.

sanctification to the Holy Spirit. Yet all these attributes are common, and belong equally to the whole Trinity.

The human mind by itself could never have come to the knowledge of the Trinity for it is a strict supernatural mystery revealed only by Christ: "Go therefore and make disciples of all nations, baptizing them in the name of the Father and of the Son and of the Holy Spirit" (Mt 28:19). Nevertheless, there exist many "proofs", both natural and supernatural, which attest at least to the existence of one all-powerful God:

I. *The Argument from Cause*: There exists no effect without a cause; there exists no created thing without a creator. The existence of the cause-and-effect relation in the world is irresistibly and intuitively evident to the human mind. Things caused are contingent, that is, dependent upon their causes. Nothing can exist without a sufficient reason for its existence. Furthermore, things caused must be traced back to a first efficient cause which is uncaused. If A comes from B, and B from C, and C from D, and so on, then ultimately one must arrive at a first cause which is itself uncaused and therefore self-existent. This uncaused cause is God.

II. *The Argument from Motion*: Motion is any activity that can be exercised by a finite being either bodily or spiritual. It includes, for example, such acts as walking, eating, growing, understanding, and decision-making. More precisely, it involves a movement from potentiality to actuality, as when a being has the capacity to do or receive something and that capacity is realized in fact. Motion being an established fact, there follows the universally true dictum that "whatever is moved is moved by something other than itself." This "something other" must be traced back ultimately to a first mover who is itself unmoved. This first mover is God.

III. *The Argument from Design*: A picture suggests an artist, a house a builder. Consequently, the existence of the visible universe with its regular and perfect order reasonably suggests the existence of a higher Being as its creator: "For all men who were ignorant of God were foolish by nature; and they were unable from the good things that are seen to know him who exists, nor did they recognize the craftsman while paying heed to his works" (Wis. 13:1). Likewise, St Paul: "Ever since the creation of the world his invisible nature, namely, his eternal power and deity, has been clearly perceived in the things that have been made. So they are without excuse" (Rom. 1:20).

IV. *Voice of conscience*: All human beings possess within their minds a conscience that speaks to them affirming that certain actions are morally good and that others are morally evil. This 'voice' of conscience is a written law likewise implanted in our natures by the superior hands of God: "They show that what the law requires is written on their hearts, while their conscience also bears witness and their conflicting thoughts accuse or perhaps excuse them" (Rom. 2:15).

V. *Revelation*: Revelation directly coming from God gives us the most complete and certain knowledge of Him. Revelation includes everything God has made known to us through the angels, the Patriarchs, the Prophets and, most importantly, Our Lord Jesus Christ Himself: "In many and various ways God spoke of old to our fathers by the prophets; but in these last days he has spoken to us by a Son" (Heb. 1:1-2).

The Fathers

Aristides of Athens, *Apology to the Emperor Hadrian Caesar* **1 & 4 (c. AD 140)**
"When I saw that the world and all that is in it is moved by a force, I understood that He who moves and maintains it is God; for whatever moves something is stronger than that which is moved, and whatever maintains something is stronger than that which is maintained. I call the One who constructed all things and maintains them God: He that is without beginning and eternal, immortal and lacking nothing, and who is above all passions and failings such as anger and forgetfulness and ignorance and the rest ... Let us proceed, then, O King, to the elements themselves, so that we may demonstrate concerning them that they are not gods, but corruptible and changeable things, produced out of the non-existent by Him that is truly God, who is incorruptible and unchangeable and invisible."

St Irenaeus of Lyons, *Against Heresies* 2, 13, 3 (c. AD 180)
"Far removed is the Father of all from those things which operate among men, the affections and the passions. He is simple, not composed of parts, without structure, altogether like and equal to Himself alone. He is all mind, all spirit, all thought, all intelligence, all reason, all ear, all eye, all light, all fountain of every good; and this is the manner in which the religious and the pious are accustomed to speak of God."

Tertullian, *Against Marcion* 1, 18, 2 (inter AD 207-212)
"It is our definition that God must be known first from nature, and afterwards He is authenticated from instruction: by nature, from His works; by instruction, from His revelations."

Minucius Felix, *The Octavius* 18, 4 (inter AD 218-235)
"If upon entering some home you saw that everything there was well-tended, neat and decorative, you would believe that some master was in charge of it, and that he was himself much superior to those good things. So too in the home of this world, when you see providence, order, and law in the heavens and on earth, believe that there is a Lord and author of the universe, more beautiful than the stars themselves and ... the whole world."

St Cyril of Jerusalem, *Catechetical Lectures* 4, 5 (c. AD 350)
"This Father of our Lord Jesus Christ is not circumscribed in any place, nor is He less than the heavens ... He knows beforehand the things that shall be, and is mightier than all. He knows all, and does as He will. He is not subject to the consequences of events, neither to astrological geniture, nor to chance, nor to fate. He is in all things perfect, and possesses equally every absolute of virtue, neither diminishing nor decreasing, but remains ever the same and unchanging."

The Roman Catechism (1566)

Pt. I, Ch. I: The meaning of the above words is this: I believe with certainty, and without a shadow of doubt profess my belief in God the Father, the First Person of the Trinity, who by His omnipotence created from nothing and preserves and governs the heavens and the earth and all things which they contain; and not only do I believe in Him from my heart and profess this belief with my lips, but with the greatest ardor and piety I tend towards Him, as the supreme and most perfect good.

Catechism of the Catholic Church (1992)

No. 199: "I believe in God": this first affirmation of the Apostles' Creed is also the most fundamental. The whole Creed speaks of God, and when it also speaks of man and of the world it does so in relation to God. The other articles of the Creed all depend on the first, just as the remaining Commandments make the first explicit. The other articles help us to know God better as he revealed himself progressively to men ...

No. 200: The confession of God's oneness, which has its roots in the divine revelation of the Old Covenant, is inseparable from the profession of God's existence and is equally fundamental. God is unique; there is only one God: "The Christian faith confesses that God is one in nature, substance, and essence."

No. 201: To Israel, his chosen, God revealed himself as the only One: "Hear, O Israel: The LORD our God is one LORD; and you shall love the LORD your God with all your heart, and with all your soul, and with all your might." Through the prophets, God calls Israel and all nations to turn to him, the one and only God: "Turn to me and be saved, all the ends of the earth! For I am God, and there is no other ... To me every knee shall bow, every tongue shall swear. 'Only in the LORD, it shall be said of me, are righteousness and strength'."

No. 202: Jesus himself affirms that God is "the one Lord" whom you must love "with all your heart, and with all your soul, and with all your mind, and with all your strength." At the same time Jesus gives us to understand that he himself is "the Lord." To confess that Jesus is Lord is distinctive of Christian faith. This is not contrary to belief in the One God. Nor does believing in the Holy Spirit as "Lord and giver of life" introduce any division into the One God:

> We firmly believe and confess without reservation that there is only one true God, eternal, infinite (*immensus*) and unchangeable, incomprehensible, almighty, and ineffable, the Father and the Son and the Holy Spirit; three persons indeed, but one essence, substance or nature entirely simple (Lateran Council IV).

Creator of Heaven and Earth

"In the beginning God created the heavens and the earth" (Gen. 1:1).

It is in the book of Genesis that we find recorded the account of Creation. St John writes in the first chapter of his Gospel: "all things were made through him, and without him was not anything made that was made" (1:3). We are told that the world did not always exist, but was created in time. The visible universe, all living things, angels and men, sprang into being: "Let them praise the name of the Lord! For he commanded and they were created" (Ps. 148:5).

God made all things, heaven and earth, out of nothing (*"Ex nihilo"*) by His Word. A creator is one who makes a thing out of nothing. Only God can create, all other things are creatures. It is fundamental that we believe in creation, out of nothing, of heaven and earth by one Almighty personal God whose power now sustains His creation (Fourth Lateran and First Vatican Councils). In an era where science purports to advance at the expense of religion, it remains obligatory for Catholics to reject any notion or theory that excludes God from being the author of all matter and life.

God had no necessity to create the universe but, being infinitely good, He wished to impart some of His goodness to created beings. St Bonaventure explains that God created all things "not to increase His glory, but to show it forth." The First Vatican Council elaborates:

> This one, true God, of His own goodness and 'almighty power', not for increasing His own beatitude, nor for attaining His perfection, but in order to manifest this perfection through the benefits which He bestows on creatures, with absolute freedom of counsel 'and from the beginning of time, made out of nothing both orders of creatures, the spiritual and the corporeal ...'

According to philosophers, God's Intellect contemplates His own Essence and understands the infinite ways in which it can be imitable in creatures. The natures of all beings are therefore dependent on God's own Essence and hence are said to belong to the *Essential Order*. Whether God brings such creatures into existence depends on His Will. All creatures created by God are said to belong to the *Existential Order*.

All creatures are made in the likeness of God. Everything created by God in some way or another reflects one or more of His infinite perfections. Hence, in opposition to Gnosticism in its various historic forms, all created things are good in themselves: "And God saw everything that he had made, and behold, it was very good" (Gen. 1:31). God cannot create anything that is essentially evil, for that would be contrary to His own essential goodness.

The Existential Order of creatures is as follows: (i) minerals; (ii) plants; (iii) animals; (iv) humans; and (v) angels. Each subsequent level is a higher order of creation possessing and reflecting more of God's own infinite perfections. Minerals possess no life; plants possess vegetative life; animals possess vegetative and sensitive life; humans possess vegetative, sensitive and intellective life; angels, being pure spirits without a body, possess intellective life greatly superior to humans. While all creatures are made in the likeness of God, humans and angels are both in the *image and likeness* of God by virtue of possessing an intellect and will to understand and love like Him.

After creating the universe, God did not abandon it to mere chance but by His power continued to preserve and govern it. He has a care for all things and directs them to the end for which He created them: "because he himself made both small and great, and he takes thought for all alike"; "For thou lovest all things that exist, and hast loathing for none of the things which thou hast made, for thou wouldst not have made anything if thou hadst hated it" (Wis. 6:7; 11:24).

However, if God is good and directs all things, why is there so much sin and misery in the world? The existence of sin is not due to the creating hand of God but to our own malice in rejecting God and turning to creatures. God forbids sin, yet permits its existence because of the certainty that a greater good will flow from it. For example, Adam's fall, as tragic as it was for him and all his posterity, was the occasion for the Word to become flesh and dwell among us: "*O happy fault, which merited such a Redeemer.*" God uses threats to deter us from sin and grace to avoid it, but leaves us to exercise our free will as we choose.

As for sufferings, persecutions, afflictions, etc., these God also permits for our good: "Good things and bad, life and death, poverty and wealth, come from the Lord" (Sir. 11:14). God desires the sinner to acknowledge the chastisement and change his ways that he may not perish everlastingly. He would wean and purify the just man from the world that he may abound in merit and receive in heaven the reward due to his patient suffering.

The Fathers

The Shepherd of Hermas, Mandate 1, 1 (inter AD 140-155)
"Believe first of all that God is one, that He created all things and set them in order, and brought out of non-existence into existence everything that is, and that He contains all things while He Himself is uncontained."

St Irenaeus of Lyons, *Against Heresies* 4, 20, 1 (c. AD 180)
"God had no need of others to make what He had already determined of Himself to make, as if He had not His own hands. For with Him always are the Word and the Wisdom, the Son and the Spirit, through whom and in whom He had made all things freely and spontaneously; and to whom He spoke, saying: 'Let us make man in our image and likeness.'"

St Theophilus of Antioch, *To Autolycus* 2, 4 (c. AD 181)
"And what great thing were it, if God made the world out of existing matter? Even a human artist, when he obtains material from someone, makes of it whatever he pleases. But the power of God is made evident in this, that he makes out of what does not exist whatever He pleases; and the giving of life and movement belongs to none other, but to God only."

Origen, *Fundamental Doctrines* 2, 9, 6 (inter AD 220-230)
"God, the Creator of all things, is good and just and almighty. He, when in the beginning He created those things which He wished to create, that is, rational beings, had no other cause for creating them except on account of Himself, that is, His own goodness."

St Augustine of Hippo, The City of God *Bk. 11, Ch. 24 (ante AD 418)*
"But in that place where it is said: 'God saw that it is good', it is sufficiently indicated that God created what He did create, not because of any necessity nor to supply for any need of His own, but solely by reason of goodness, that is, because He is good."

The Roman Catechism (1566)

Pt. I, Ch. II: For God formed the world not from materials of any sort, but created it from nothing and that not by constraint or necessity, but spontaneously, and of His own free will. Nor was He impelled to create by any other cause than a desire to communicate His goodness to creatures. Being essentially happy in Himself, He stands not in need of anything; as David expresses it: *I have said to the Lord, thou art my God, for thou hast no need of my goods.*

Catechism of the Catholic Church (1992)

No. 290: "In the beginning God created the heavens and the earth": three things are affirmed in these words of Scripture: the eternal God gave a beginning to all that exists outside of himself; he alone is Creator (the verb "create" – Hebrew *bara* – always has God for its subject). The totality of what exists (expressed by the formula "the heavens and the earth") depends on the One who gives it being.

No. 295: We believe that God created the world according to his wisdom. It is not the product of any necessity whatever, nor of blind fate or chance. We believe that it proceeds from God's free will, he wanted to make his creatures share in his being, wisdom, and goodness: "For you created all things, and by your will they existed and were created." Therefore the Psalmist exclaims: "O LORD, how manifold are your works! In wisdom you have made them all ..."; and "The LORD is good to all, and his compassion is over all that he has made."

No. 300: God is infinitely greater than all his works: "You have set your glory above the heavens." Indeed, God's "greatness is unsearchable." But because he is the free and sovereign Creator, the first cause of all that exists, God is present to his creatures' inmost being: "In him we live and move and have our being." In the words of St Augustine, God is "higher than my highest and more inward than my innermost self."

Creator of Heaven and Earth: Angels

"... a thousand thousands served him, and ten thousand times ten thousand stood before him" (Dan. 7:10).

Angels are the highest and most perfect of God's creatures, being pure spirits endowed with power, intelligence and free will. They surround the throne of God and are "His ministers that do his will" (Ps. 103:21).

God created the angels before men, and in a state of innocence and grace together with excellent gifts. But God created them also free and capable of sinning and willed that they should undergo a trial in order to merit heaven permanently as a reward for their fidelity. What the exact test was, is not known to us.

Lucifer together with one-third of the other angels rebelled against God's plan and, becoming devils with perverted wills, they were cast into hell: "God did not spare the angels when they sinned" (2 Pet. 2:4). There they will remain forever, without repentance or redemption, having given free and full consent to their rebellion and knowing the consequences thereof. In other words, they permanently fixed their own end.

Though they have no physical body like humans, angels have the power to appear in bodily form. This they can do in one of either two ways. They can "assume bodies" by manipulating matter to create and put on a mask in the same way humans can put on a disguise. This is the case when angels are seen by more than one person at a time. The other way is by placing an image within a person's imagination that gives the impression that there is a body there. This is normally the case when only one person is having a purely private experience of an angel.[1]

---

[1] See Peter Kreeft, *Angels (and Demons), What do we Really Know About Them?*, Ignatius Press, 1995, p. 52.

The exact number of angels is not stated in Scripture, however, according to the Prophet Daniel, "... a thousand thousands served him, and ten thousand times ten thousand stood attending him" (Dan. 7:10).

According to the Fathers of the Church, the angels are divided into three hierarchies, and each hierarchy into three choirs:

(i) Seraphim, Cherubim, Thrones.
(ii) Dominations, Principalities, Powers.
(iii) Virtues, Archangels, Guardian Angels.

Only three of the heavenly host are known to us by name:

(i) Gabriel ("Strength of God").
(ii) Michael ("Who is like unto God").
(iii) Raphael ("Remedy of God").

Though condemned to hell, demons are permitted by God to come upon the earth to test mankind: "Your adversary the devil prowls around like a roaring lion, seeking some one to devour" (1 Pet. 5:8). In their envy and hatred they try to lead us to sin, and can even affect our bodies by possession. Nevertheless, "God is faithful, and he will not let you be tempted beyond your strength, but with the temptation will also provide the way of escape, that you may be able to endure it" (1 Cor. 10:13). If then we are overcome, the fault is our own.

The chief occupation of the good angels is to adore and to praise God continually: "Day and night without ceasing they sing, 'Holy, holy, holy, is the Lord God Almighty" (Rev. 4:8). Angels also, as God's ministers, take part in the government of the universe, executing the Divine commands: "Are they not all ministering spirits sent forth to serve, for the sake of those who are to obtain salvation?" (Heb. 1:14).

It is the Church's teaching that each person has a Guardian Angel appointed by God as a special protector: "See that you do not despise one of these little ones; for I tell you that in heaven their angels always behold the face of my Father who is in heaven" (Mt 18:10); "And when he knocked at the door of the gateway, a maid named Rhoda came to answer. Recognizing Peter's voice, in her joy she did not open the gate but ran in and told that Peter was standing at the gate. They said to her,

'You are mad.' But she insisted that it was so. They said, 'It is his angel'" (Acts 12:13-15).

St Michael was the special protector of Israel and is now venerated as the guardian of God's Church against the wickedness and snares of the devil.

We should love and revere the angels, and with confidence recommend ourselves to them in all the circumstances of our lives.

The Fathers

The Shepherd of Hermas, Visions 3, 4, 1 (inter AD 140-155)

"I answered and said to her: 'Lady, this is a great and wonderful thing. But the six young men who are building, who are they, lady?' 'These are the holy angels of God, who were the first to be created, and to whom the Lord entrusted all of His creation, to increase it and to build it up, and to be masters of the whole of creation. Through them, therefore, the building of the tower will be completed.' 'But the others, who are bringing the stones: – who are they?'

'They also are holy angels of God; but these six are superior to them. The building of the tower, then, shall be completed; and all alike shall rejoice around the tower, and shall give glory to God, because the building of the tower was accomplished.'"

Tertullian, *Apology* 22, 4 (AD 197)

"The business (of the fallen angels, who are the demons) is to corrupt mankind. Thus, from the very first, spiritual wickedness augured man's destruction. Therefore do they inflict diseases and other grievous misfortunes upon our bodies; and upon the soul they do violence to achieve sudden and extraordinary excesses. Their marvelous subtlety and elusiveness give them access to both parts of man's substance ... Therefore are they everywhere in a moment. The whole world is but one place to them. What and where anything happens they can know and tell with equal facility."

Clement of Alexandria, *Miscellanies* 6, 13, 107, 2 (post AD 202)
"Even here in the Church the gradations of bishops, presbyters, and deacons happen to be imitations, in my opinion, of the angelic glory and of that arrangement which, the Scriptures say, awaits those who have followed in the footsteps of the Apostles, and who have lived in perfect righteousness according to the Gospel."

Origen, *Fundamental Doctrines* 1, Preface, 6 (inter AD 220-230)
"In regard to the devil and his angels and opposing powers, the ecclesiastical teaching maintains that these beings do indeed exist; but what they are or how they exist is not explained with sufficient clarity. This opinion, however, is held by most: that the devil was an angel; and having apostatized, he persuaded as many angels as possible to fall away with himself; and these, even to the present time, are called his angels."

St Hilary of Poitiers, *Commentaries on Psalms [Ps. 130 (129)]*, 7 (c. AD 365)
"We recall that there are many spiritual powers, to whom the name angels is given, or presidents of Churches. There are, according to John, angels of the Churches of Asia. And there were, as Moses bears witness, when the sons of Adam were separated, bounds appointed for the peoples according to the number of the angels. And, as the Lord teaches, there are for little children, angels who see God daily. There are, as Raphael told Tobias, angels assisting before the majesty of God, and carrying to God the prayers of suppliants. Mention is made of all this, because you might wish to understand these angels as the eyes, or the ears, or the hands, or the feet of God."

St Gregory Nazianzus, *Second Theological Oration* 28, 31 (AD 380)
"We know that there are certain Angels and Archangels, Thrones, Dominations, Principalities, Powers, Splendors, Ascents, Intelligent Virtues or Intelligences, natures pure and unalloyed; immovable to evil, or so moved only with difficulty; circling ever in chorus around the First Cause."

The Roman Catechism (1566)

Pt. I, Ch. II: Moreover, He created out of nothing the spiritual world and Angels innumerable to serve and minister to Him; and these He enriched and adorned with the admirable gifts of His grace and power ... That the devil and the other rebel angels were gifted from the beginning of their creation with grace, clearly follows from these words of the Sacred Scriptures: *He* (the devil) *stood not in the truth.* On this subject St Augustine says: *In creating the angels He endowed them with good will, that is, with pure love that they might adhere to Him, giving them existence and adorning them with grace at one and the same time. Hence we are to believe that the holy Angels were never without good will, that is, the love of God.*

Catechism of the Catholic Church (1992)

No. 329: St Augustine says: "'Angel' is the name of their office, not of their nature. If you seek the name of their nature, it is 'spirit'; if you seek the name of their office, it is 'angel': from what they are, 'spirit', from what they do, 'angel.'" With their whole beings the angels are *servants* and messengers of God. Because they "always behold the face of my Father who is in heaven" they are the "mighty ones who do his word, hearkening to the voice of his word."

No. 336: From its beginning until death, human life is surrounded by their watchful care and intercession. "Beside each believer stands an angel as protector and shepherd leading him to life." Already here on earth the Christian life shares by faith in the blessed company of the angels and men united in God.

No. 392: Scripture speaks of a sin of these angels. This "fall" consists in the free choice of these created spirits, who radically and irrevocably rejected God and his reign. We find a reflection in that rebellion in the tempter's words to our first parents: "You will be like God." The devil "has sinned from the beginning..."; he is "a liar and the father of lies."

Creator of Heaven and Earth: Man

"So God created man in his own image, in the image of God he created him; male and female he created them" (Gen. 1:27).

God then "breathed into his nostrils the breath of life; and man became a living being" (Gen. 2:7). Man was also given dominion over all the other creatures upon earth.

However, in the plan of God He saw that it was not good for Adam to be alone for he needed companionship with one like himself. So God sent a deep sleep upon Adam, and while he was sleeping took one of his ribs and from it created Eve whom God gave to Adam as his companion and helpmate. Beholding his new partner for the first time Adam was ecstatic and exclaimed, "This at last is bone of my bones and flesh of my flesh; she shall be called Woman, because she was taken out of Man" (Gen. 2:23).

Being made in the image and likeness of God, Adam and Eve possessed the spiritual powers of intellect and will. They were created in a state of innocence and happiness, and enriched with supernatural (above nature) gifts to elevate, or "divinize", them and so enable them to participate in the life of God. These gifts included sanctifying grace with the concomitant infused theological virtues of faith, hope and charity, the infused moral virtues of prudence, justice, fortitude and temperance, the seven gifts of the Holy Spirit, and the uncreated grace of the indwelling of the Blessed Trinity. Through such gifts, Adam and Eve possessed the sonship of God and the right to inherit heaven. In addition to these supernatural gifts, Adam and Eve possessed preternatural (beyond nature) gifts to perfect them as human beings, namely, impassibility, immortality, integrity and infused knowledge. Their lower instincts, or passions, obeyed their reason and their reason obeyed God. All these were gifts freely given by God, above our natural rights.

God placed Adam and Eve in the paradise of Eden, a garden of delights, where they would live in happiness and innocence, growing in grace, until God transported them body and soul to heaven for all eternity. However, it was God's determination for Adam and Eve to merit heaven through obedience and so He put them to the test: "And the Lord God commanded the man, saying, 'You may freely eat of every tree of the garden; but of the tree of the knowledge of good and evil you shall not eat, for in the day that you eat of it you shall die'" (Gen. 2:16-17). Satan in the form of a serpent approached Eve: "you will be like God" (Gen. 3:5). Adam, puffed up with pride at the prompting of Eve, sought inordinately to become like God in knowledge, and then believing God to be a liar, disobeyed His prohibition and ate of the Tree of Knowledge.

At once, Adam and Eve felt shame and wished to hide from God's presence. The punishments were then pronounced. They lost the sonship of God by being stripped of sanctifying grace and hence their right to enter heaven. Four wounds opened up within them: malice in the will; ignorance in the intellect; concupiscence in the concupiscible appetite; and debility in the irascible appetite. Their minds were now darkened, and they became prone to evil, disorder and weakness. They were driven out of Paradise, angels guarding the entrances with flaming swords to prevent their return and access to the Tree of Life. Toil and sickness were henceforth to be their lot, and with the forfeiture of the gifts of impassibility and immortality they became subject to pain, suffering, sickness and death: "In the sweat of your face you shall eat bread till you return to the ground, for out of it you were taken; you are dust, and to dust you shall return" (Gen. 3:19).

Through the disobedience of Adam and Eve "sin came into the world through one man and death through sin, and so death spread to all men because all men sinned" (Rom. 5:12). The miserable consequences of Adam's sin were to pass from him to all his posterity through natural generation, a fatal stain upon our souls. To this, the Church gives the term "original sin": "we were by nature children of wrath" (Eph. 2:3).

God in His mercy, however, would not allow humanity to remain in this fallen state. Satan would not be allowed any victory through envy and deception. God gave us time for repentance, and promised a new Adam and Eve who would co-operate together to redeem our lost innocence and regain the kingdom of heaven (Gen. 3:15).

The Fathers:

Tatian the Syrian, *Address to the Greeks* 15 (inter AD 165-175)
"It is necessary for us now to seek what once we had, but have lost: indeed, to unite the soul with the Holy Spirit, and to strive after union with God ... The perfect God is without flesh; but man is flesh ... Such is the form of man's constitution: and if it be like a temple, God desires to dwell in it through the Spirit, His Representative; but if it be not such a habitation, then man excels the beasts only in that he has articulate speech, and in other respects his manner of life is like theirs and he is not a likeness of God."

St Irenaeus of Lyons, *Against Heresies* 5, 3, 2 (c. AD 180)
"God, taking soil from the earth, made man. And surely it is much more difficult and more incredible that from non-existent bones and nerves and veins and the rest of the human system, he makes him to exist, and in fact raises him up as an animated and rational living being ..."

Tertullian, *The Soul* 22, 2 (inter AD 208-212)
"We define the soul as born of the breath of God, immortal, corporal (sic), having form, simple in substance, acquiring knowledge by its own operation, showing itself in various ways, free to choose, subject to misfortunes, changeable according to natural inclinations, rational, the mistress, she who divines, descended from a single source."

St Cyprian of Carthage, *The Advantage of Patience* 19 (AD 256)
"The devil bore impatiently the fact that man was made in the image of God; and that is why he was the first to perish and the first to bring others to perdition. Adam, contrary to the heavenly command, was impatient in regard to the deadly food, and fell into death; nor did he preserve, under the guardianship of patience, the grace he received from God."

The Roman Catechism (1566)

Pt. I, Ch. II: Lastly, He formed man from the slime of the earth, so created and constituted in body as to be immortal and impassible, not, however, by the strength of nature, but by the bounty of God. Man's soul He created to His own image and likeness; gifted him with free will, and tempered all his motions and appetites so as to subject them, at all times, to the dictates of reason. He then added the admirable gift of original righteousness, and next gave him dominion over all other animals.

Catechism of the Catholic Church (1992)

No. 396: God created man in his image and established him in his friendship. A spiritual creature, man can live this friendship only in free submission to God ...

No. 397: Man, tempted by the devil, let his trust in his Creator die in his heart and, abusing his freedom, disobeyed God's command. This is what man's first sin consisted of.

No. 400: The harmony in which they had found themselves, thanks to original justice, is now destroyed: the control of the soul's spiritual faculties over the body is shattered; the union of man and woman becomes subject to tensions, their relations henceforth marked by lust and domination. Harmony with creation is broken: visible creation has become alien and hostile to man. Because of man, creation is now subject "to its bondage to decay." Finally, the consequence explicitly foretold for this disobedience will come true; man will "return to the ground" for out of it he was taken. Death makes its entrance into human history.

And in Jesus Christ, His only Son, Our Lord

"For God so loved the world that he gave his only Son, that whoever believes in him should not perish but have eternal life" (Jn 3:16).

"I will put enmity between you and the woman, and between your offspring and hers; he shall bruise your head, and you shall bruise his heel" (Gen. 3:15). These words constitute what is known as the *Protoevangelium*, the first Gospel, or promise of a Redeemer to come. This promise formed the essential heart and hope of the religion of the Jews of the Old Testament: "Truly I tell you, many prophets and righteous men longed to see what you see, and did not see it, and to hear what you hear, and did not hear it" (Mt 13:17).

As the sin of Adam and Eve offended the infinite dignity of God, the satisfaction due to God in atonement needed to be of infinite value. However, no mere creature could make such a satisfaction since no creature, however holy or exalted, could offer more than a finite reparation. There was a necessity, therefore, for the Redeemer to be both God and man – man, that he might suffer and die on our behalf; God, that an infinite merit might attach to His atonement. Such a Redeemer was sent by God – Jesus Christ, the Incarnate Word, the Second Person of the Blessed Trinity: "For there is one God, and there is one mediator between God and men, the man Christ Jesus, who gave himself as a ransom for all" (1 Tim. 2:5).

"But when the time had fully come, God sent forth his Son, born of woman, born under the law, to redeem those who were under the law, so that we might receive adoption as sons" (Gal. 4:4-5). God the Son became the man Jesus Christ: "And the Word became flesh and dwelt among us" (Jn 1:14). The Latin word for *'incarnation'* means "to put on flesh." Christ could not have become Redeemer of humanity without a human nature, for it was His assumed human nature that was the instrumental cause of our salvation. In therefore voluntarily giving her flesh to the Son of God, the Virgin Mary in the most intimate way co-operated to bring into effect God's plan of redemption.

Jesus Christ is not only truly God, begotten of the Father in all eternity, but also truly man from the time He was conceived in His Mother's womb: "who, though he was in the form of God, did not count equality with God a thing to be grasped, but emptied himself, taking the form of a servant, being born in the likeness of men" (Phil. 2:6-7). Thus, Christ has the divine and a human nature united in His one Divine Person – this union is called the *Hypostatic Union*, "hypostatic" meaning person in Greek. This union will never be dissolved, and remains so today. When Our Lord's body lay in the Sepulcher, the Person of the Word still remained united to it, just as it remained united to His soul in Abraham's Bosom (1 Pet. 3:19).

As Christ has the divine and a human nature, so also has He the divine and a human will. Yet His human will is ever in perfect accord with His divine will: "if it be possible, let this cup pass from me; nevertheless, not as I will, but as thou wilt" (Mt 26:39). Likewise, Christ possesses both the divine and a human intellect. In His *divine* intellect, Christ possesses comprehensive knowledge of all things past, present and future, as well as the infinite array of possibilities. On earth, in His *human* intellect, by virtue of the Hypostatic Union, Christ enjoyed the *beatific vision* in which he had the immediate vision of God. This knowledge was not infinite, but as great as His created human intellect could receive. In that vision, He beheld all things past, present and future. He also possessed *infused* knowledge of all things related to His mission, as well as *acquired, or experimental* knowledge through His external senses.

Being the Second Person of the Blessed Trinity, Jesus Christ is truly the Son of God: "thou art my Son, today I have begotten thee" (Heb. 1:5). For many, the thought that God can have a Son who has the same nature as Himself is anathema. Yet, Christ is not a separate God, but a distinct Person, God's image of Himself: "He is the image of the invisible God, the first-born of all creation" (Col. 1:15). Jesus Christ is the only Son of God by nature, whereas we become through Christ the sons of God by adoption: "For you did not receive the spirit of slavery to fall back into fear, but you have received the spirit of sonship. When we cry, 'Abba! Father!'" (Rom. 8:15). This adoption formally begins with baptism, which infuses into our souls the indelible mark of a Christian, or *character*, and incorporates us into Christ's Body, the Church.

The name "Jesus" means "God saves." The title "Christ" means

"Anointed." Jesus' name is one of power and confidence, and should invoke our deepest respect. It has always be part of Catholic piety to reverence the name of Jesus when hearing it pronounced: "... at the name of Jesus every knee should bow, in heaven and on earth and under the earth, and every tongue confess that Jesus Christ is Lord, to the glory of God the Father" (Phil. 2:10-11).

Jesus Christ has the threefold character of *Priest, Prophet* and *King*. He is a priest in once having offered Himself on Calvary for the redemption of the world, and continuing to offer Himself daily in the Mass: "Thou art a priest for ever, after the order of Melchizedek" (Heb. 5:6); He is a Prophet by being a teacher of truth, revealing the mysteries of God and foretelling of things to come: "The Lord God will raise up for you a prophet like me from among you, from your brethren – him you shall heed" (Deut. 18:15-16); He is King because He is God Himself and He came down to earth to establish His Church, a spiritual kingdom over which He shall rule for all eternity: "King of kings and Lord of lords" (Rev. 19:16).

Jesus Christ is Our Lord and Lord of all because He created all things in the universe: "... all things were made through him, and without him was not anything made that was made" (Jn 1:3). Furthermore, we owe all entirely to Him for having redeemed us "at a great price" and freeing us from the slavery of sin and the devil. How great then should our love, respect and obedience be to such a Lord, seeing that it is to Him that we owe all that we possess!

The Fathers

St Ignatius of Antioch, *Letter to the Ephesians* **Address (AD 110)**
"Ignatius, also called Theophorus, to the Church at Ephesus in Asia ... united and chosen through true suffering by the will of the Father in Jesus Christ our God ... There is one Physician, who is both flesh and spirit, born and not born, who is God in man, true life in death, born both of Mary and from God, first able to suffer and then unable to suffer, Jesus Christ our Lord ... For our God, Jesus Christ, was conceived by Mary in accord with God's plan: of the seed of David, it is true, but also of the Holy Spirit ..."

St Justin Martyr, *First Apology* 13 (c. AD 155)
"Our teacher of these things, born for this end, is Jesus Christ, who was crucified under Pontius Pilate, the procurator in Judea in the time of Tiberius Caesar. We will prove that we worship Him reasonably; for we have learned that He is the Son of the True God Himself, that He holds a second place, and the spirit of Prophecy a third. For this they accuse us of madness, saying that we attribute to a crucified man a place second to the unchangeable and eternal God, the Creator of all things; but they are ignorant of the mystery which lies therein."

Tertullian, *Apology* 21, 6 (AD 197)
"So also, that which proceeds from God is God and Son of God, and both are one. Likewise, as He is Spirit from Spirit, and God from God, He is made a second by count and in numerical sequence, but not in actual condition; for He comes forth from the source but does not separate therefrom."

St Athanasius, *On the Incarnation of the Word of God Against the Arians* 21 (c. AD 365)
"And when (Christ) says, 'Father, if it be possible, let this chalice pass from Me; yet, not My will be done, but Yours'; and 'the spirit is ready, but the flesh is weak', He gives evidence therein of two wills, the one human, which is of the flesh, and the one divine, which is of God. That which is human, because of the weakness of the flesh, shrinks from suffering. That, however, which is divine, is ready."

The Roman Catechism (1566)

Pt. I, Ch. III: The human race, having fallen from its elevated dignity, no power of men or Angels could raise it from its fallen condition and replace it in its primitive state. To remedy the evil and repair the loss it became necessary that the Son of God, whose power is infinite, clothed in the weakness of our flesh, should remove the infinite weight of sin and reconcile us to God in His blood.

Catechism of the Catholic Church (1992)

No. 432: The name "Jesus" signifies that the very name of God is present in the person of his Son, made man for the universal and definitive redemption from sins. It is the divine name that alone brings salvation, and henceforth all can invoke his name, for Jesus united himself to all men through his Incarnation, so that "there is no other name under heaven given among men by which we must be saved."

No. 436: The word "Christ" comes from the Greek translation of the Hebrew *Messiah*, which means "anointed." It became the name proper to Jesus only because he accomplished perfectly the divine mission that "Christ" signifies ...

No. 449: By attributing to Jesus the divine title "Lord", the first confessions of the Church's faith affirm from the beginning that the power, honor, and glory due to God the Father are due also to Jesus, because "he was in the form of God", and the Father manifested the sovereignty of Jesus by raising him from the dead and exalting him into his glory.

Who was Conceived by the Holy Spirit, Born of the Virgin Mary

"... when the time had fully come, God sent forth his Son, born of woman, born under the law" (Gal. 4:4).

The Prophet Isaiah had foretold the birth of Christ to King Ahaz in the eighth century BC: "Behold, a virgin shall conceive and bear a son, and his name shall be called Emmanuel (i.e., God with us)" (Mt 1:23).

When the time decreed by God the Father for sending Christ into the world had arrived, the Archangel Gabriel was sent from heaven to obtain the consent of Mary. During their conversation the Archangel said: "The Holy Spirit will come upon you, and the power of the Most High will overshadow you; therefore the child to be born will be called holy, the Son of God" Our Lady's response came without hesitation: "Behold, I am the handmaid of the Lord; let it be to me according to your word." Seeing that Our Lady had given her full and total consent to being the Mother of God, the Archangel Gabriel then left her (Lk 1:35-38). At that instant, without any detriment to her spotless virginity, Our Lady miraculously conceived within her womb the Savior of the world.

Just as there was a co-operation between Adam and Eve in humanity's fall, likewise was there to be in God's plan a co-operation between the new Adam and Eve in humanity's redemption. For without Our Lady's free consent to be the mother of the Messiah, the Word of God would not have received the necessary human nature to redeem Adam and all his posterity. Our Lady's obedience therefore became the cause of salvation for the whole of humanity, undoing the damage caused by Eve's disobedience. Hence, does the Church appropriately bestow upon Her the title of the "New Eve." As the Fathers proclaim, "Death through Eve: Life through Mary."

At this time, Our Lady and St Joseph were living in Nazareth, yet it had been foretold that Bethlehem was to be the Messiah's birthplace: "But you, O Bethlehem Ephrathah, who are little to be among the clans of Judah, from you shall come forth for me one who is to be ruler in Israel" (Mich. 5:2). By a special providence of God, a decree was issued by Augustus Caesar for a census of "all the world." In obedience, Our Lady and St Joseph, both being of the Royal House of David, traveled to Bethlehem, the City of David. Here, Our Lady gave birth to Jesus Christ, while a multitude of the heavenly host proclaimed: "Glory to God in the highest, and on earth peace among men with whom he is pleased!" (Lk 2:10-14).

The third Joyful Mystery of the Most Holy Rosary invites us to meditate on the nativity of Christ. The fruit of this Mystery is poverty of spirit. One can understand why this virtue was chosen when considering the circumstances of Christ's birth. The Holy Family had to content themselves with no better than a poor stable occupied by an ox and an ass, exposed to the open air, with the Child Jesus wrapped in swaddling clothes and laid in a manger of straw. Poverty was to be the lot of Christ His entire life. He was born in a manger that belonged to another, and was buried in a tomb that belonged to another.

The Catholic Church dogmatically asserts that Our Lady was a virgin before, during, and remained so perpetually after the birth of Christ (*Ante partum, In partu, Post partum*). As a consequence, the very act of giving birth to Christ was not detrimental to Our Lady's virginity. It is a pious belief that Christ proceeded from His Mother's womb in the same way He was later to proceed from the tomb, that is, by passing through the rock without rolling it away (Mt 28:2).

In giving birth to Christ, we may truly say that the Virgin Mary became the Mother of God. The error known as Nestorianism argued in the early fifth century that, as Our Lady supplied only Christ's human and not divine nature, She could only be called *Christotokos* (Mother of Christ), not *Theotokos* (Mother of God). Nestorianism had its foundation in an erroneous Christology that asserted that Christ was two separate persons, one human and one divine, rather than one divine person with two natures, human and divine, united hypostatically. When Our Lady gave her flesh to Christ she was clothing a divine person. In giving birth to Christ she was giving birth to a divine person. Christ is God, therefore

Our Lady is truly the Mother of God. Scripture itself attests to this:

"And why is this granted me, that the mother of my Lord should come to me?" (Lk 1:43).

"On the third day there was a wedding at Cana of Galilee, and the mother of Jesus was there ..." (Jn 2:1).

"... standing by the cross of Jesus were his mother ..." (Jn 19:25).

And what of St Joseph? He was chosen to be the protector of Our Lady's virginity, to defend her from accusations after the birth of her Son, to assist the Holy Family in their flight to Egypt, to be the guardian and foster-father of Christ, and to have the Son of God obedient to him. Scripture speaks little of St Joseph except that he was "a just man" (Mt 1:19). The modern devotion to St Joseph was strongly promoted by the great Spanish mystic and reformer St Teresa of Avila: "Knowing from experience the amazing influence that St Joseph has with God, I would persuade everybody to honor him with special devotion. Every year on St Joseph's feast I ask for some special favor and I have had my desires fulfilled." St Joseph has also been particularly honored by the Church as the Patron Saint of a happy death, for he had the most happy death by having Our Lord and Our Lady at his side. He is also invoked as the Patron Saint of workers, and Pope Pius IX in 1870 declared him Patron of the Universal Church.

The Fathers

St Ignatius of Antioch, *Letter to the Ephesians* **18, 2 (c. AD 110)**
"For our God, Jesus Christ, was conceived by Mary in accord with God's plan: of the seed of David, it is true, but also of the Holy Spirit. He was born and baptized so that by His submission He might purify the water. The virginity of Mary, her giving birth, and also the death of the Lord, were hidden from the prince of this world: – three mysteries loudly proclaimed, but wrought in the silence of God."

St Justin Martyr, *Dialogue with Trypho the Jew* 100 (c. AD 155)
"He became Man by the Virgin so that the course which was taken by disobedience in the beginning through the agency of the serpent, might be also the very course by which it would be put down. For Eve, a virgin and undefiled, conceived the word of the serpent, and bore disobedience and death. But the Virgin Mary received faith and joy when the angel Gabriel announced to her the glad tidings that the Spirit of the Lord would come upon her and the power of the Most High would overshadow her, for which reason the Holy One being born of her is the Son of God. And she replied: 'Be it done unto me according to thy word'."

St Irenaeus of Lyons, *Against Heresies* 3, 22, 4 (c. AD 180)
"(Eve) having become disobedient, was made the cause of death for herself and for the whole human race; so also Mary, betrothed to a man but nevertheless still a virgin, being obedient, was made the cause of salvation for herself and for the whole human race ... Thus, the knot of Eve's disobedience was loosed by the obedience of Mary. What the virgin Eve had bound in unbelief, the Virgin Mary loosed through faith."

St Ephrem of Edessa, *Songs of Praise* 1, 1; 1, 2 (ante AD 373)
"Awake, my harp, your songs in praise of the Virgin Mary! Lift up your voice and sing the wonderful history of the Virgin, the daughter of David, who gave birth to the Life of the World. Who loves you is amazed and who would understand is silent and confused, because he cannot probe the Mother who gave birth in her virginity. If it is too great to be clarified with words the disputants ought not on that account cross swords with your Son."

The Roman Catechism (1566)

Pt. I, Ch. IV: As the body of Christ was formed of the pure blood of the immaculate Virgin without the aid of man, as we have already said, and by the sole operation of the Holy Ghost, so also, at the moment of His Conception, His soul was enriched with an overflowing fullness of the Spirit of God, and a superabundance of all graces. For God gave not to Him, as to others adorned with holiness and grace, His Spirit by measure, as St John testifies, but poured into His soul the plenitude of all graces so abundantly that *of his fullness we all have received.*

Catechism of the Catholic Church (1992)

No. 484: The Annunciation to Mary inaugurates "the fullness of time", the time of the fulfillment of God's promises and preparations. Mary was invited to conceive him in whom the "whole fullness of deity" would dwell "bodily." The divine response to her question, "How can this be, since I know not man?" was given by the power of the Spirit: "The Holy Spirit will come upon you."

No. 495: Called in the Gospels "the mother of Jesus", Mary is acclaimed by Elizabeth, at the prompting of the Spirit and even before the birth of her Son, as "the mother of my Lord." In fact, the One whom she conceived as man by the Holy Spirit, who truly became her Son according to the flesh, was none other than the Father's eternal Son, the second person of the Holy Trinity. Hence the Church confesses that Mary is truly "Mother of God" (*Theotokos*).

No. 504: Jesus is conceived by the Holy Spirit in the Virgin Mary's womb because he is the New Adam, who inaugurates the new creation: "The first man was from the earth, a man of dust; the second man is from heaven." From his conception, Christ's humanity is filled with the Holy Spirit, for God "gives him the Spirit without measure." From "his fullness" as the head of redeemed humanity "we have all received, grace upon grace."

Suffered Under Pontius Pilate, was Crucified, Died and was Buried

"He was despised and rejected by men; a man of sorrows, and acquainted with grief" (Is. 53:3).

The great mission of Our Lord Jesus Christ was to redeem the world, to reconcile humanity to an offended God and restore us to His friendship. To achieve this, Our Lord had to satisfy the Divine Justice for our sins - He had to suffer and die in our place.

As the Son of God, every act of Our Lord was an act of a divine person. Therefore, every single act of suffering on Christ's part, every drop of His Precious Blood spilt, was of infinite value and therefore sufficiently meritorious to redeem humanity. Yet, for love of us, Christ of His own free will chose to place no human limit on His suffering, pouring out His Blood to the very last drop. In the Book of Isaiah we find the mysterious prophecy of the suffering and death of the Messiah:

"Who has believed what we have heard? And to whom has the arm of the Lord been revealed? For he grew up before him like a young plant, and like a root out of dry ground; he had no form or comeliness that we should look at him, and no beauty that we should desire him. He was despised and rejected by men; a man of sorrows, and acquainted with grief; and as one from whom men hide their faces he was despised, and we esteemed him not. Surely he has borne our griefs and carried our sorrows; yet we esteemed him stricken, smitten by God, and afflicted. But he was wounded for our transgressions, he was bruised for our iniquities; upon him was the chastisement that made us whole, and with his stripes we are healed. All we like sheep have gone astray; we have turned every one to his own way; and the Lord has laid on him the iniquity of us all. He was oppressed, and he was afflicted, yet he opened not his mouth; like a lamb that is led to the slaughter, and like a sheep that before its shearers is dumb, so he opened not his mouth ..." (Is. 53:1-7).

From the Gospels we can list specifically the cruel sufferings endured by Christ that ended in His terrible and ignominious death:

I. The agony in the Garden of Gethsemani when His sweat became as drops of blood as He submitted to the will of His Father.

II. His betrayal by Judas, and His abandonment by the other disciples who were His closest confidants during the past three years.

III. The denials of St Peter, the head of the other Apostles and the one who had previously sworn publicly to defend Our Lord.

IV. The false accusations before the High Priests, Herod and Pilate, as well as the mockery, scorn and derision poured upon Him in the process.

V. His condemnation to death on the basis of false evidence, as well as the cowardice and injustice of Pilate.

VI. His rejection in favor of the murderer Barabbas by a mob incited by Christ's enemies, which drowned out His supporters.

VII. His scourging at the pillar by two executioners each using a 'cat-of-nine-tails' lined with hooks and carrying metal balls at the end of each lash.

VIII. The crown of thorns pressed over the whole of His head, and the derision He suffered as a mock king.

IX. The heavy Cross placed upon and opening up a wound in His shoulder, and the painful journey to Calvary.

X. His clothes being torn off Him brutally, re-opening the dried wounds caused by the scourging.

XI. The nailing of His hands and feet to the Cross with nails several inches in length.

XII. His bleeding and dying on the Cross for three hours, between two thieves, while enduring further mockery and derision.

XIII. The mysterious sensation of being abandoned even by His Heavenly Father.

XIV. The bitter taste of the sponge dipped in vinegar.

XV. His death on the Cross (which was followed by the piercing of His right side with a lance that penetrated into His heart, causing blood and water to gush forth).

This sacrifice of His life, Christ offered on the altar of the Cross as priest and victim to His Father for the salvation of the world: "he is the expiation for our sins, and not for ours only but also for the sins of the whole world" (1 Jn 2:2); "you were bought with a price" (1 Cor. 6:20).

By His death on the Cross, Christ merited for us the adoption of sons and the right to inherit the kingdom of heaven. However, not all will receive such an inheritance: "and being made perfect he became the source of eternal salvation to all who obey him" (Heb. 5:9). We are required to believe with sincerity, observe the Commandments, pray regularly and frequent the sacraments, practise good works, and repent of our actual sins.

The sufferings of Christ are the most striking proof of His great love for us. It is for this reason that the Church in all Her prayers and ceremonies makes such frequent use of the Sign of the Cross. Tertullian, at the end of the second century, testifies that it was the common practice of Christians to imprint the Sign of the Cross on their foreheads in all their everyday actions. It has always been the sign that distinguishes Christ's followers, a sign of contradiction to the devil and all his followers, a sign that speaks of victory over the enemies of our salvation: *"In Hoc Signo Vinces"* (In this sign you will conquer).

The Fathers

St Ignatius of Antioch, *Letter to the Smyrnaeans* 1, 1 (c. AD 110)
"You are confirmed in love by the Blood of Christ, firmly believing in regard to our Lord that He is truly of the family of David according to the flesh, and God's Son by the will and power of God, truly born of a Virgin, baptized by John so that all justice might be fulfilled by Him, in the time of Pontius Pilate and Herod the Tetrarch truly nailed in the flesh on our behalf ..."

Letter of Barnabas 7, 2 (inter AD 117-132)
"If, then, the Son of God, being the Lord and destined to judge the living and the dead, suffered so that His being wounded might make us live, let us believe that the Son of God could not suffer, except for our sake."

Origen, *Homilies on Numbers* Hom. 24, 1 (post AD 244)
"If there had been no sin, there would have been no necessity for the Son of God to become a lamb; nor would it have been necessary for Him to take flesh and be slain. He would have remained that which He was from the beginning, the Word of God ... in all these sacrificial victims there was one lamb who was able to take away sin from the whole world. Therefore have other victims ceased to be, because this victim was such that, although one alone, he sufficed for the salvation of the whole world."

St Hilary of Poitiers, *Commentaries on the Psalms* [On Ps. 54 (53)] (c. AD 365)
"We have declared repeatedly and without cease that it was the only-begotten Son of God who was crucified, and that He was condemned to death: He that is eternal by reason of the nature which is His by His birth from the eternal Father; and it must be understood that He underwent the passion not from any natural necessity, but for the sake of the mystery of man's salvation; and that His submitting to the passion was not from His being compelled thereto, but of His own will ... God suffered, therefore, because He voluntarily submitted Himself to the passion."

St Gregory of Elvira, *Homilies on the Books of Sacred Scripture* 2 (inter AD 365-385)
"The tree of the cross, clearly represents an image which to some seems as hard and rough as wood, because on it the Lord was hung so that our sins, which came to us from the tree of transgression, might be punished by being affixed-again, it is through the same Man – to the tree of the cross ... To others it stands for shade and refreshment, because believers are protected from the heat and rigor of persecution, and there refreshed."

The Roman Catechism (1566)

Pt. I, Ch. V: Should anyone inquire why the Son of God underwent His most bitter Passion, he will find that besides the guilt inherited from our first parents, the principal causes were the vices and crimes which have been perpetrated from the beginning of the world to the present day and those which will be committed to the end of time. In His Passion and death the Son of God, our Savior, intended to atone for and blot out the sins of all ages, to offer for them to His Father a full and abundant satisfaction.

Catechism of the Catholic Church (1992)

No. 599: Jesus' violent death was not the result of chance in an unfortunate coincidence of circumstances, but is part of the mystery of God's plan, as St Peter explains to the Jews of Jerusalem in his first sermon on Pentecost: "This Jesus (was) delivered up according to the definite plan and foreknowledge of God." This Biblical language does not mean that those who handed him over were mere passive players in a scenario written in advance by God.

No. 613: Christ's death is both the *Paschal sacrifice* that accomplishes the definitive redemption of men, through "the Lamb of God, who takes away the sin of the world," and the *sacrifice of the New Covenant*, which restores man to communion with God by reconciling him to God through the "blood of the covenant, which was poured out for many for the forgiveness of sins."

No. 617: The Council of Trent emphasizes the unique character of Christ's sacrifice as "the source of eternal salvation" and teaches that "his most holy Passion on the wood of the cross merited justification for us." And the Church venerates his cross as it sings: "Hail, O Cross, our only hope."

He Descended into Hell, the Third Day He Rose Again from the Dead

"The Son of man is to be delivered into the hands of men, and they will kill him, and he will be raised on the third day" (Mt 17:22-23).

At the moment of Our Lord's death, His soul descended into that part of hell otherwise known as the *Limbo of the Patriarchs* or *Abraham's Bosom* – the place where the souls of the Just who died before Christ were detained: "For as Jonah was three days and three nights in the belly of the whale, so will the Son of man be three days and three nights in the heart of the earth" (Mt 12:40). Christ announced the glad tidings of redemption to them, and their approaching admission into heaven with Him on Ascension Day: "he went and preached to the spirits in prison" (1 Pet. 3:19). Our Lord's very presence transformed Limbo into a delightful paradise, as we gather from His words to the Good Thief: "Truly, I say to you, today you will be with me in Paradise" (Lk 23:43).

It is also an expressed opinion that Christ visited purgatory, to console and comfort the souls suffering there: "I will penetrate to all the lower parts of the earth, and will behold all that sleep, and will enlighten all that hope in the Lord" (Sir. 24:45).

For three days Christ's soul was separated from His body, yet His divinity was never for a moment separated from either. On the third day, Christ, by His own divine power, reunited His soul to His body and rose again immortal and impassible: "Destroy this temple, and in three days I will raise it up" (Jn 2:19); "I lay down my life, that I may take it again" (Jn 10:17).

After His resurrection, Christ retained in His body the marks of His sufferings: "Put your finger here, and see my hands; and put out your hand, and place it in my side; do not be faithless, but believing" (Jn 20:27). These marks will ever remain to show that He rose again in the same body, and as tokens of His victory over sin and death.

Moreover, having risen with the same but glorified body, Christ is no longer subject to death, as were those He miraculously raised to life. Furthermore, He is the principle and cause of the future general resurrection of all the dead: "For as in Adam all die, so also in Christ shall all be made alive" (1 Cor. 15:22).

On the fact of the resurrection rests our belief in Christianity: "if Christ has not been raised, then our preaching is in vain and your faith is in vain ..." (1 Cor. 15:14). There are eleven accounts given in Scripture of Christ's appearances after His resurrection:

I. To St Mary Magdalene near the Sepulcher while she was looking for Christ's body (Jn 20:16).
II. To the holy women returning from the Sepulcher after being shown the empty tomb by the angel (Mt 28:9).
III. To Simon Peter alone as head of the Apostles (Lk 24:34).
IV. To the two disciples on the road to Emmaus to whom Christ expounded all the Scriptures concerning Himself from Moses and the Prophets (Lk 24:25).
V. To the Apostles assembled behind locked doors, excepting St Thomas, on the first Easter Sunday (Jn 20:21).
VI. A week later to all of the Apostles behind the same locked doors, including St Thomas (Jn 20:28).
VII. To St Peter and six other Apostles while they were fishing fruitlessly upon the Sea of Galilee (Jn 21:7).
VIII. To the eleven Apostles in Galilee upon a mountain where Christ had bidden them meet him (Mt 28:16).
IX. More than five hundred of the brethren together (1 Cor. 15:6).
X. To St James the Less as recounted by St Paul (1 Cor. 15:7).
XI. On the day of His ascension from Mount Olivet (Acts 1:9).

The Apostles were to go on and preach Christ's resurrection before the very Jewish leaders who put Him to death. They preached this truth to an incredulous world, filled with the unction of the Holy Spirit, braving persecution, imprisonment and death: "And we bring you the good news that what God promised to the fathers, this he has fulfilled to us their children by raising Jesus" (Acts 13:32-33).

The Fathers

St Irenaeus of Lyons, *Against Heresies* 5, 31, 2 (c. AD 180)
"For since the Lord went away into the midst of the shadow of death where the souls of the dead were, and afterwards arose in the body, and after the resurrection was taken up, it is clear that the souls also of His disciples, on account of which the Lord underwent these things, will go away into the place allotted them by God."

St Cyril of Jerusalem, *Catechetical Lectures* 4, 11 (c. AD 350)
"(Christ) descended into the subterranean regions so that He might ransom from there the just ... David was there, and Samuel, and all the Prophets; and John, the same who, through his messengers, said: 'Are You the one who is to come, or shall we look for another?' Would you not want Him to go down to free such men as these?"

St Gregory of Nyssa, *The Great Catechism* 1 (post AD 383)
"God (the Son) did not impede death from separating His soul from His body according to the necessary order of nature, but has reunited them to one another in the resurrection, so that He Himself might be, in His person, the meeting point for death and life, by arresting in Himself the decomposition of nature produced by death and so becoming the source of reunion for the separated parts."

St Augustine of Hippo, *Explanation of the Psalms* 120, 4 (c. AD 392-418)
"It is no great thing to believe that Christ died. This the pagans, Jews, and all the wicked believe; in a word, all believe that Christ died. But that He rose from the dead is the belief of Christians. To believe that He rose again, this we deem of great moment."

The Roman Catechism (1566)

Pt. I, Ch. VI: Finally, the Resurrection of our Lord, as the pastor should inculcate, was necessary to complete the mystery of our salvation and redemption. By His death Christ liberated us from sin; by His

Resurrection, He restored to us the most important of those privileges which we had forfeited by sin. Hence these words of the Apostle: *He was delivered up for our sins, and rose again for our justification.* That nothing, therefore, may be wanting to the work of our salvation, it was necessary that as He died, He should also rise again.

Catechism of the Catholic Church (1992)

No. 632: The frequent New Testament affirmations that Jesus was "raised from the dead" presuppose that the crucified one sojourned in the realm of the dead prior to his resurrection. This was the first meaning given in the apostolic preaching to Christ's descent into hell: that Jesus, like all men, experienced death and in his soul joined the others in the realm of the dead. But he descended there as Savior, proclaiming the Good News to the spirits imprisoned there.

No. 639: The mystery of Christ's resurrection is a real event, with manifestations that were historically verified, as the New Testament bears witness. In about AD 56, St Paul could already write to the Corinthians: "I delivered to you as of first importance what I also received, that Christ died for our sins in accordance with the Scriptures, and that he was buried, that he was raised on the third day in accordance with the Scriptures, and that he appeared to Cephas, then to the Twelve ..." The Apostle speaks here of the living tradition of the Resurrection which he had learned after his conversion at the gates of Damascus.

He Ascended into Heaven; is Seated at the Right Hand of God the Father Almighty

"So then the Lord Jesus, after he had spoken to them, was taken up into heaven, and sat down at the right hand of God" (Mk 16:19).

After His resurrection, Christ returned to His Apostles and "presented himself alive after his passion by many proofs, appearing to them during forty days, and speaking of the kingdom of God" (Acts 1:3). During these forty days, Christ laid the foundations for the Church He was to leave behind by bestowing on His Apostles all that was necessary for them to continue His work of salvation in the world:

(i) "... opened their minds to understand the scriptures" (Lk 24:45), that is, He illuminated the Apostles as to how He fulfilled the myriad prophecies in the Old Testament which foretold His coming.

(ii) He gave them the power to forgive sins: "If you forgive the sins of any, they are forgiven; if you retain the sins of any, they are retained" (Jn 20:23). This power was in addition to the power of binding and loosing already given to St Peter specifically in Matt. 16 and to the other Apostles collectively in Matt. 18.

(iii) He confirmed St Peter as the visible Head of His Church on earth: "Feed my lambs ... Tend my sheep" (Jn 21:15-16). Here, the promise made by Our Lord in Matt. 16:18ff. to make St Peter the rock-foundation of the Church was fulfilled.

(iv) He commissioned the Apostles to carry His Gospel to the very ends of the earth and bring all peoples into the one flock under one shepherd: "Go therefore and make disciples of all nations, baptizing them in the name of the Father and of the Son and of the Holy Spirit them to observe all that I have commanded you; and lo, I am with you always, to the close of the age" (Mt 28:19-20).

The Apostles' Creed

On the fortieth day after His Resurrection, Christ led His Apostles to Bethany and the Mountain of Olives. After imparting the above blessing, He raised Himself up, and as He ascended He took with Him all the Souls of the Just who had been waiting in the Bosom of Abraham: "And when he had said this, as they were looking on, he was lifted up, and a cloud took him out of their sight" (Acts 1:9).

Many have surmised whether it would have been more opportune if Christ had remained visibly on earth after His resurrection to continue the work of salvation Himself. However, it was necessary for Our Lord to ascend into heaven for the following reasons:

(i) To take possession of that glory due to Him as man: "he humbled himself and became obedient unto death, even death on a cross. Therefore God has highly exalted him and bestowed on him the name which is above every name" (Phil. 2:8-9).

(ii) To be our mediator with God the Father: "Christ Jesus, who died, yes, who was raised from the dead, who is at the right hand of God, who indeed intercedes for us" (Rom. 8:34); "if any one does sin, we have an advocate with the Father, Jesus Christ the righteous" (1 Jn 2:1).

(iii) To prepare a place for us: "In my Father's house are many rooms; if it were not so, would I have told you that I go to prepare a place for you? And when I go and prepare a place for you, I will come again and will take you to myself, that where I am you may be also" (Jn 14:2-3).

(iv) To send the Holy Spirit: "it is to your advantage that I go away, for if I do not go away, the Counselor will not come to you; but if I go, I will send him to you" (Jn 16:7).

When Scripture speaks of Christ sitting "at the right hand of God" the words are used in a figurative sense, meaning that Christ, as God, is equal in all things to the Father and, as man, holds an exalted position above all the Angels and Saints: "he raised him from the dead and made him sit at his right hand in the heavenly places, far above all rule and authority and power and dominion, and above every name that is named, not only in this age but also in that which is to come" (Eph. 1:20-21).

The Fathers

St Irenaeus of Lyons, *Against Heresies* 5, 31, 2 (c. AD 180)
"For since the Lord went away into the midst of the shadow of death where the souls of the dead were, and afterwards arose in the body, and after the resurrection was taken up, it is clear that the souls also of His disciples, on account of which the Lord underwent these things, will go away into the place allotted them by God."

Tertullian, *The Demurrer Against the Heretics* 13, 1 (c. AD 200)
"Thenceforth He preached a new law and a new promise of the Kingdom of heaven; worked miracles; was crucified, rose again on the third day; and having ascended into heaven, sat at the right of the Father; and sent the Holy Spirit with vicarious power to lead those who believe."

St Leo I, *Sermons* 73, 4 (ante AD 461)
"There was great and indescribable cause for rejoicing when, in the sight of the holy multitude, above the dignity of all heavenly creatures, the nature of the human race went up, to surpass the ranks of Angels and to rise beyond the heights of the Archangels, to have its being uplifted limited by no sublimity until, received to sit with the eternal Father, it was associated on the throne of His glory, to whose nature it was joined in the Son."

St John Damascene, *The Source of Knowledge* 4, 2 (AD 743)
"By 'the Father's right hand' we understand the glory and honor of divinity, where he who exists as Son of God before all ages, indeed as God, of one being with the Father, is seated bodily after he became incarnate and his flesh was glorified."

The Roman Catechism (1566)

Pt. I, Ch. VII: He also ascended into heaven in order to teach us to follow Him thither in mind and heart. For as by His death and Resurrection He bequeathed to us an example of dying and rising again in spirit, so by His Ascension He teaches and instructs us that though dwelling on earth, we should raise ourselves in desire to heaven, confessing that we are *pilgrims and strangers on the earth*, seeking a country and that we are *fellow-citizens with the saints, and the domestics of God*, for, says the same Apostle, *our conversation is in heaven.*

Catechism of the Catholic Church (1992)

No. 659: "So then the Lord Jesus, after he had spoken to them, was taken up into heaven, and sat down at the right hand of God." Christ's body was glorified at the moment of his Resurrection, as proved by the new and supernatural properties it subsequently and permanently enjoys. But during the forty days when he eats and drinks familiarly with his disciples and teaches them about the kingdom, his glory remains veiled under the appearance of ordinary humanity. Jesus' final apparition ends with the irreversible entry of his humanity into divine glory, symbolized by the cloud and by heaven, where he is seated from that time forward at God's right hand. Only in a wholly exceptional and unique way would Jesus show himself to Paul "as to one untimely born", in a last apparition that established him as an apostle.

From Thence He Shall Come to Judge the Living and the Dead

"This Jesus, who was taken up from you into heaven, will come in the same way as you saw him go into heaven" (Acts 1:11).

At the last day Jesus Christ shall come again with great power and glory to judge all mankind: "When the Son of man comes in his glory, and all the angels with him, then he will sit on his glorious throne. Before him will be gathered all the nations, and he will separate them one from another ... And they will go away into eternal punishment, but the righteous into eternal life" (Mt 25:31-46).

As to when the Day of Judgment will be we do not know. Many have attempted to specify a date, even the precise hour. Such people pore over the Scriptures looking for clues or hidden codes, especially the Book of Daniel and St John's Revelation. However, Scripture itself makes it clear that "But of that day and hour no one knows, not even the angels of heaven, nor the Son, but the Father only" (Mt 24:36). Nevertheless, there will be many signs preceding this momentous event:

(i) Wars and chastisements plaguing the nations to a degree unheralded in recorded history: "For nation will rise against nation, and kingdom against kingdom, and there will be famines and earthquakes in various places" (Mt 24:7).
(ii) The Church, once the mustard seed, has by this time spread out its limbs across the world giving all the birds the opportunity to nest in its branches (Mt 13:31): "And this gospel of the kingdom will be preached throughout the whole world, as a testimony to all nations; and then the end will come" (Mt 24:14).
(iii) Heresy, schism and apostasy will be rampant in a world which has heard but rejected the Gospel: "For false Christs and false prophets will arise and show great signs and wonders, so as to

lead astray, if possible, even the elect" (Mt 24:24).
(iv) As a punishment for its apostasy, the world will be allowed to be seduced by the greatest of all deceivers, the Antichrist: "Let no one deceive you in any way; for that day will not come, unless the rebellion comes first, and the man of lawlessness is revealed, the son of perdition" (2 Thes. 2:3).
(v) Confusion, fear and a sense of doom will grip the nations: "And there will be signs in sun and moon and stars, and upon the earth distress of nations in perplexity at the roaring of the sea and the waves, men fainting with fear and with foreboding of what is coming on the world; for the powers of the heavens will be shaken. And then they will see the Son of man coming in a cloud with power and great glory" (Lk 21:25-27).

When the Day of Judgment comes the Lord "will bring to light the things now hidden in darkness and will disclose the purposes of the heart" (1 Cor. 4:5); "I tell you, on the day of judgment men will render account for every careless word they utter" (Mt 12:36); "and all were judged by what they had done" (Rev. 20:13). St Paul exhorts all Christians to be on guard, leading just lives for the coming of this great day: "establish your hearts unblamable in holiness before our God and Father, at the coming of our Lord Jesus with all his saints" (1 Thes. 3:13).

The dealings of God with each individual shall also be made manifest and be acknowledged by all men; all souls in heaven, purgatory and hell will be united with their glorious or darkened bodies; the complete reward or punishment of each individual will be revealed to all others: "The heavens declare his righteousness, for God himself is judge!" (Ps. 50:6).

All those who have lived and died on earth from the creation of Adam to the Day of Judgment shall attend the Judgment. Christ shall sit as Judge in the Valley of Jehoshaphat: "I will gather all the nations and bring them down to the valley of Jehoshaphat, and I will enter into judgment with them there" (Joel 3:2); "And he will send out his angels with a loud trumpet call, and they will gather his elect from the four winds, from one end of heaven to the other" (Mt 24:31). He, who on earth was despised, calumnied, rejected and given a criminal's execution on a cross, shall be glorified before humanity as the Lord of all.

The Fathers

The So-Called Second Letter of Clement of Rome to the Corinthians 1, 1 (c. AD 150)
"Brethren, we think of Jesus Christ as God and as the Judge of the living and the dead."

St Justin Martyr, *First Apology* 53 (c. AD 155)
"Why should we believe a crucified man, that He is the Firstborn of the unbegotten God, and that He will pass judgment on the whole human race, if we had not found testimonies published about Him before He came and was made Man, and if we had not seen these predictions fulfilled?"

St Hippolytus of Rome, *Against the Greeks* 3 (ante AD 225)
"Standing before (Christ's) judgment, all of them, men, angels, and demons, crying out in one voice, shall say: 'Just is your judgment!' And the justice of that cry will be apparent in the recompense made to each. To those who have done well, everlasting enjoyment shall be given; while to the lovers of evil shall be given eternal punishment."

St Cyprian of Carthage, *The Lapsed* 17 (AD 251)
"The Lord alone is able to have mercy. He alone, who bore our sins, who grieved for us, and whom God delivered up for our sins, is able to grant pardon for the sins which have been committed against Him ... Certainly we believe that the merits of the martyrs and the works of the just will be of great avail with the Judge – but that will be when the day of judgment comes, when, after the end of this age and of the world, His people shall stand before the tribunal of Christ."

St Cyril of Alexandria, *Against the Anthropomorphites* 16 (post AD 441)
"The Divine Scripture says that the judgment is to take place after the resurrection of the dead. But the resurrection is not to take place until Christ returns to us from heaven in the glory of the Father with the holy angels ... Since, therefore, Christ the Savior of all has not yet come down from heaven, neither has the resurrection taken place, nor has

compensatory action been visited upon any ... so that those who possess the wealth of this world might know that if they do not wish to be liberal and generous and social, and choose to come to assist the needs of the poor, they will be overtaken by a terrible and inevitable punishment."

The Roman Catechism (1566)

Pt. I, Ch. VIII: Besides, it was right that the just should be encouraged by the hope, the wicked appalled by the terror, of a future judgment; so that knowing the justice of God the former should not be disheartened, while the latter through fear and expectation of eternal punishment might be recalled from the paths of vice. Hence, speaking of the last day, our Lord and Savior declares that a general judgment will one day take place, and He describes the signs of its approach, that seeing them, we may know that the end of the world is at hand. At His Ascension also, to console His Apostles, overwhelmed with grief at His departure, He sent angels, who said to them: *This Jesus who is taken up from you into heaven, shall so come, as you have seen him going into heaven.*

Catechism of the Catholic Church (1992)

No. 673: Since the Ascension Christ's coming in glory has been imminent, even though "it is not for you to know times or seasons which the Father has fixed by his own authority." This eschatological coming could be accomplished at any moment, even if both it and the final trial that will precede it are "delayed."

No. 675: Before Christ's second coming the Church must pass through a final trial that will shake the faith of many believers. The persecution that accompanies her pilgrimage on earth will unveil the "mystery of iniquity" in the form of a religious deception offering men an apparent solution to their problems at the price of apostasy from the truth. The supreme religious deception is that of the Antichrist, a pseudo-messianism by which man glorifies himself in place of God and of his Messiah come in the flesh.

No. 678: Following in the steps of the prophets and John the Baptist, Jesus announced the judgment of the Last day in his preaching. Then will the conduct of each one and the secrets of hearts be brought to light. Then will the culpable unbelief that counted the offer of God's grace as nothing be condemned. Our attitude about our neighbor will disclose acceptance or refusal of grace and divine love. On the last day Jesus will say: "Truly I say to you, as you did it to one of the least of these my brethren, you did it to me."

I Believe in the Holy Spirit

"And I will pray the Father, and he will give you another Counselor, to be with you for ever..." (Jn 14:16).

The Holy Spirit is a distinct person yet the same Lord and God as the Father and the Son. During the period of theological heresies that racked the early Church, the divinity of the Holy Spirit was specifically denied, particularly by Macedonius of Constantinople, compelling the Church to add the words *"the Lord, the giver of life ... with the Father and the Son He is worshipped and glorified"* into the Nicene Creed. Scripture contains ample passages that testify both to the distinct personality of the Holy Spirit and His mission of sanctification:

"... why has Satan filled your heart to lie to the Holy Spirit ... How is it that you have contrived this deed in your heart? You have not lied to men but to God" (Acts 5:3-4).

"Likewise the Spirit helps us in our weakness ... the Spirit intercedes for the saints according to the will of God" (Rom. 8:26-27).

"And do not grieve the Holy Spirit of God, in whom you were sealed for the day of redemption" (Eph. 4:30).

In the Church's language, the Son is said to be *begotten* of the Father, while the Holy Spirit *proceeds* from the Father and the Son as from a single principle. According to the western Fathers, the Son is the mental Word of God, or God's own knowledge of Himself. The Father contemplates and knows Himself in the Word while the Word simultaneously contemplates and knows the Father. What follows from this mutual knowledge is mutual love, or the *Holy Spirit*. However, in all this there is nothing that is before or after, nothing that is greater or less: the Father, Son and Holy Spirit are eternal and equal in every respect.

Scripture attributes distinct divine qualities to the Holy Spirit:
(i) Omniscience, or knowledge of all things: "For the Spirit searches everything, even the depths of God" (1 Cor. 2:10).
(ii) Omnipotence, or possession of all power: "The Holy Spirit will come upon you, and the power of the Most High will overshadow you" (Lk 1:35).
(iii) Omnipresence, or having presence everywhere: "Whither shall I go from thy Spirit? Or whither shall I flee from thy presence?" (Ps. 139:7).

Various names are given to the Holy Spirit: Third Person of the Blessed Trinity; the Holy Ghost; the Paraclete; the Comforter; the Sanctifier; Advocate; Gift of the Most High; Giver of Life; Spirit of Truth; Spirit of Love. Many other titles can be found in Sacred Scripture and the Church's tradition. As the Holy Spirit has various names, so has He appeared visibly in different forms: in the form of a dove at Our Lord's baptism (Mt 3:16); as a shining cloud at Christ's Transfiguration (Mt 17:5); and as tongues of fire on Pentecost Day (Acts 2:3). The cloud upon which Christ ascended into heaven was also the Holy Spirit.

Invisibly, the Holy Spirit actively abides and works in the souls of the Just: "He who believes in me, as the scripture has said, 'Out of his heart shall flow rivers of living water.' Now this he said about the Spirit, which those who believed in him were to receive; for as yet the Spirit had not been given, because Jesus was not yet glorified" (Jn 7:38-39); "If a man loves me, he will keep my word, and my Father will love him, and we will come to him and make our home with him" (Jn 14:23); "Do you not know that you are God's temple and that God's Spirit dwells in you?" (1 Cor. 3:16). The Holy Spirit works in our souls to animate and fill them with the true fire of love, cleansing them from sin and making them holy and pleasing to God: "were washed, you were sanctified, you were justified in the name of the Lord Jesus Christ and in the Spirit of our God" (1 Cor. 6:11).

Apart from Himself, the Holy Spirit places into the soul sanctifying grace with the concomitant infused theological virtues of faith, hope and charity, the infused moral virtues of prudence, justice, fortitude and temperance and the seven gifts of the Holy Spirit (wisdom, understanding, knowledge, fortitude, counsel, piety and fear of the Lord).

Saint Catherine of Siena was permitted by God to see a soul in a state of sanctifying grace and told her confessor, "Oh! If you could but see the beauty of a soul in a state of grace, you would sacrifice your life a thousand times for its salvation ... It is the image and likeness of God in that soul, and Divine grace which make it so beautiful."

The descent of the Holy Spirit upon the Apostles on Pentecost Day is considered to be birthday of the Church. Beforehand, the Apostles had been weak and timid, dull and ignorant. Afterwards, armed with the gift of tongues, they fearlessly went forth and proclaimed Christ in all languages: "... And they were all filled with the Holy Spirit and began to speak in other tongues, as the Spirit gave them utterance" (Acts 2:4). The effects of their preaching were immediate and dramatic. St Peter in one sermon alone converted three thousand: "And the Lord added to their number day by day those who were being saved" (Acts 2:41; 47).

In this way we witness the beginnings of that visible society of men known as the Catholic Church, and it is by virtue of the Holy Spirit that the Apostles will strengthen and govern the Church: "But the Counselor, the Holy Spirit, whom the Father will send in my name, he will teach you all things, and bring to your remembrance all that I have said to you" (Jn 14:26); "Take heed to yourselves and to all the flock, in which the Holy Spirit has made you overseers, to care for the church of the Lord which he obtained with the blood of his own" (Acts 20:28). Until the end of time the Catholic Church will be protected by the Holy Spirit, enabling it to withstand all crises, so that "the powers of death shall not prevail."

The Fathers

Athenagoras of Athens, *Supplication for the Christians* **10 (c. AD 177)**
"The Holy Spirit also, who works in those who speak prophetically, we regard as an effluence of God, flowing out and returning like a ray of the sun. Who, then, would not be astonished to hear those called atheists, who speak of God the Father and of the Son and of the Holy Spirit, and who proclaim Their power in union and Their distinction in order?"

St Irenaeus of Lyons, *Against Heresies* 4, 7, 4 (c. AD 180)

"[The Father] is ministered to in all things by His own Offspring, and by the latter's Likeness: that is, by the Son and by the Holy Spirit, by the Word and by the Wisdom, whom all the angels serve and to whom they are subject."

Tertullian, *Against Praxeas* 25, 1 (post AD 213)

"The Father and the Son are distinguished by what is proper to each. He promises to send the Paraclete also, for whom He will ask the Father, after He has ascended to the Father; and He calls the Paraclete 'another.' How it is that He is 'another' we have already explained. Further, He says, 'He will receive of what is mine,' just as He Himself had received from the Father. Thus the connection of the Father in the Son, and of the Son in the Paraclete, produces three who, though coherent, are distinct one from another. These three are one, and yet not one: for 'I and the Father are one' was said in regard to their unity of substance, but not in regard to a singularity of number."

St Hilary of Poitiers, *The Trinity* 2, 29 (inter AD 356-359)

"Concerning the Holy Spirit, however, I ought not remain silent, nor yet is it necessary to speak. Still, on account of those who do not know Him, it is not possible for me to be silent. However, it is not necessary to speak of Him who must be acknowledged, who is from the Father and the Son, His sources. Indeed, it is my opinion that there ought be no discussion about whether He exists ... I think, however, that the reason why some remain in ignorance or doubt about this, is that they see this third name, that by which the Holy Spirit is named, applied frequently also to the Father and to the Son. But there need be no objection to this, for both Father and Son are spirit and holy."

St Athanasius, *Four Letters to Serapion of Thmuis* 1, 24 (c. AD 359-360)

"We are all said to be partakers of God through the Holy Spirit. 'Do you not know,' it says, 'that you are a temple of God, and the Spirit of God dwells in you? If anyone ruins the temple of God, him will God ruin; for it is holy, this temple of God, which is just what you are.' If the Holy Spirit were a creature, there could be no communion of God with us through Him. On the contrary, we would be joined to a creature, and we would be foreign to the divine nature, as having nothing in common with it ... But if by participation in the Spirit we are made partakers in the divine nature, it is insanity for anyone to say that the Spirit has a created nature and not the nature of God."

The Roman Catechism (1566)

Pt. I, Ch. IX: Christ the Lord, speaking of the Holy Ghost, says: *He shall glorify me, because he shall receive of mine.* We also find that the Holy Ghost is sometimes called in Scripture *the Spirit of Christ*, sometimes, *the Spirit of the Father*; that He is one time said to be sent by the Father, another time, by the Son,–all of which clearly signifies that He proceeds alike from the Father and the Son. *He,* says St Paul, *who has not the Spirit of Christ belongs not to him.* In his Epistle to the Galatians he also calls the Holy Ghost the Spirit of Christ: *God hath sent the Spirit of his Son into your hearts, crying: Abba, Father.* In the Gospel of St Matthew, He is called the Spirit of the Father: *It is not you that speak, but the Spirit of your Father that speaketh in you.*

Catechism of the Catholic Church (1992)

No. 688: The Church, a communion living in the faith of the apostles which she transmits, is the place where we know the Holy Spirit:
- in the Scriptures he inspired.
- in the Tradition, to which the Church Fathers are always timely witnesses.
- in the Church's Magisterium, which he assists.
- in the sacramental liturgy, through its words and symbols, in which the Holy Spirit puts us into communion with Christ.
- in prayer, wherein he intercedes for us.
- in the charisms and ministries by which the Church is built up.
- in the signs of apostolic and missionary life.
- in the witness of saints through whom he manifests his holiness and continues the work of salvation.

No. 689: The One whom the Father has sent into our hearts, the Spirit of his Son, is truly God. Consubstantial with the Father and the Son, the Spirit is inseparable from them, in both the inner life of the Trinity and his gift of love for the world. In adoring the Holy Trinity, life-giving, consubstantial, and indivisible, the Church's faith also professes the distinction of persons. When the Father sends his Word, he always sends his Breath. In their joint mission, the Son and the Holy Spirit are distinct but inseparable. To be sure, it is Christ who is seen, the visible image of the invisible God, but it is the Spirit who reveals him.

The Holy Catholic Church

"... if I am delayed, you may know how one ought to behave in the household of God, which is the church of the living God, the pillar and bulwark of the truth" (1 Tim. 3:15).

The Holy Catholic Church is the society of the redeemed, the visible kingdom of God upon earth, comprising all baptized persons who believe and profess the teachings of Jesus Christ, and who at the same time are in communion with His representative, the Pope of Rome.

Just as there is only one God, one Lord and one Baptism, so is the Church "one and unique as a sacrament ... a sign and instrument of unity ... with the center of unity given to us by Christ in the service of Peter" (Extraordinary Synod of Bishops, *Final Report*, 1985).

It is upon the rock of St Peter and his successor, the Pope of Rome, that the stability of the Church rests: "you are Peter, and on this rock I will build my church, and the powers of death shall not prevail against it. I will give you the keys of the kingdom of heaven, and whatever you bind on earth shall be bound in heaven, and whatever you loose on earth shall be loosed in heaven" (Mt 16:18-19). Distinct controversy surrounds this passage, with many denying that Christ intended to make Simon Peter the rock on which to build His Church, or that Simon Peter was given authority of any significance. Without giving an exhaustive response, it is necessary to take note of the following facts:

I. On first beholding Simon Our Lord changed his name to *Cephas*: "So you are Simon the son of John? You shall be called Cephas (which means Peter)" (Jn 1:42). Cephas and Peter both mean *rock*. The significance of this name change cannot be ignored. It was to contrast what Simon Peter was before he met Our Lord to what he would become afterwards, that is, the firm rock on which Our Lord would build His Church.

II. In six other New Testament verses we find Simon being specifically called Cephas, or rock: 1 Cor. 1:12; 1 Cor. 3:22; 1 Cor. 9:12; 1 Cor. 15:5; Gal. 2:7 & 11 & 14.

III. If Simon Peter was given no office of significance, why did Our Lord bestow upon him the keys of the kingdom of heaven to bind and loose?: "I will give you the keys of the kingdom of heaven, and whatever you bind on earth shall be bound in heaven, and whatever you loose on earth shall be loosed in heaven" (Mt 16:19). No office held or bestowed upon man has been of such significance; and who upon earth today can legitimately claim to possess such power and authority except for St Peter's successor?

IV. The episode related in Jn 21:15 contains the fulfillment of Our Lord's promise to build His Church upon Simon Peter. It is in this episode that Our Lord asks Simon Peter whether he loves Him "more than these" and then after extracting Simon Peter's three-fold affirmation of love charges him to "Feed my lambs," "Tend my sheep," that is, tend to the spiritual needs of all the other members of Christ's Church.

The kingdom of God upon earth, being a hierarchical institution, comprises those who are to command and teach, and those who are to obey and be taught. The first comprise the bishops and priests; the second, the laity. The authority to command and teach is directly from God Himself: "Go therefore and make disciples of all nations, baptizing them in the name of the Father and of the Son and of the Holy Spirit, teaching them to observe all that I have commanded you" (Mt 28:19-20); "heed to yourselves and to all the flock, in which the Holy Spirit has made you overseers, to care for the church of the Lord" (Acts 20:28). This hierarchy, however, does not exclude legitimate forms of collaboration between clerics and the laity. In most countries today it is principally the laity who undertake tasks such as catechizing and numerous lay groups have been formed in union with the clergy with the aim of imbuing all levels of society with Christian principles. Furthermore, the laity no less than clerics are called to holiness and to preach Jesus Christ as Lord in word and deed.

Despite the fact that the Catholic Church is one and a center of unity, She possesses within Her bosom many and different Oriental (Eastern) Churches which are in communion with the See of Peter. "The Catholic Church holds in great esteem the institutions, liturgical rites, ecclesiastical traditions and discipline of Christian life of the Oriental Churches, because they are resplendent in their venerable antiquity and because in them is present the Tradition from the Apostles through the Fathers."[1]

Scripture lays upon all the strict obligation to hear and receive the teaching of the Church:

"... If he refuses to listen to them, tell it to the church; and if he refuses to listen even to the church, let him be to you as a Gentile and a tax collector" (Mt 18:17).

"He who hears you hears me, and he who rejects you rejects me, and he who rejects me rejects him who sent me" (Lk 10:16).

"Truly, truly, I say to you, he who receives any one whom I send receives me; and he who receives me receives him who sent me" (Jn 13:20).

"As the Father has sent me, even so I send you" (Jn 20:21).

"Obey your leaders and submit to them; for they are keeping watch over your souls, as men who will have to give account" (Heb. 13:17).

"...you may know how one ought to behave in the household of God, which is the church of the living God, the pillar and bulwark of the truth" (1 Tim. 3:15).

The mission of the Apostles to govern and teach was not to end with them, but was to be continued by their successors to the end of time: "... and lo, I am with you always, to the close of the age" (Mt 28:20). To believe that the written New Testament replaced the authority of the Apostles after the death of St John is to believe erroneously that the Church founded by Christ changed in Her essence. Furthermore, the Scriptures themselves show that the Apostles handed on their office through the laying of hands to subsequent generations as their successors: Acts 13:2; 1 Tim. 4:14; Tit. 1:5.

The Church must possess four "marks" in order to be truly the Church of God: *One, Holy, Catholic* and *Apostolic.*

We proclaim one Church because Christ came on earth to

---

[1] Vatican II, *Decree on Eastern Catholic Churches*, 1964, para. 1.

establish not a number of churches, but only one Church: "... and on this rock I will build my Church" (Mt 16:18); "So there shall be one flock, one shepherd" (Jn 10:16). She must be one, for "Every kingdom divided against itself is laid waste, and a divided household falls" (Lk 11:17).

The Church must be holy, having an all-holy Founder, and being designed to lead all to holiness: "in splendor, without spot or wrinkle or any such thing, that she might be holy and without blemish" (Eph. 5:27).

The Church must be catholic, because She must teach all nations, and carry on Our Lord's work to the end of time: "Go therefore and make disciples of all nations ... and lo, I am with you always, to the close of the age" (Mt 28:19-20).

The Church must be apostolic, for Her doctrines and traditions must be those of the Apostles, and Her bishops must come down from the Apostles in an unbroken succession.

These four distinctive marks are found fully united only in the Holy Catholic Church. Elements of sanctification and truth are found in varying degrees in the other Protestant denominations and these objectively constitute the basis of a certain communion. However, this communion is imperfect due to the rejection of many different articles of Catholic belief, as well as the adherence to other inconsistencies and contradictions which lead many to be "tossed to and fro and carried about with every wind of doctrine" (Eph. 4:14).

Every baptized person who professes the Catholic Faith is a member of the Catholic Church. All other baptized persons, who are in error through no fault of their own, and are in good faith, and in a state of grace, and who in all sincerity endeavor, according to their knowledge, to do God's will, are in *partial* communion with the Catholic Church.

Even the unbaptized, who are invincibly ignorant of the True Church, but have an implicit desire of submitting to Her, can attain salvation, thanks to the mediation of Christ and the Church. They even share in many of the Church's graces, but are deprived of countless other spiritual aids exclusive to the Catholic Church.

However, where a person outside the Body of the Church knows of Her and Her claims to be the Truth, or has the opportunity of knowing Her, but through indifference and neglect fails to procure this knowledge, his rejection or ignorance becomes culpable, and he is responsible to God for his neglect, etc.

When, therefore, a Catholic uses the words "I believe in the Holy Catholic Church", he professes that Jesus Christ has established a visible and infallible teaching Church, ruling with Divine authority, speaking in the Name of Her heavenly Founder, and destined to endure for all time. We must believe and obey Her, for She is in truth the One Ark of Salvation for all.

The Fathers

***The So-Called Second Letter of Clement of Rome to the Corinthians* 14, 2 (c. AD 150)**
"I presume that you are not ignorant of the fact that the living Church is the body of Christ. The Scripture says, 'God made man male and female.' The male is Christ, and the female is the Church. Moreover, the Books and the Apostles declare that the Church belongs not to the present, but has existed from the beginning. She was spiritual, just as was our Jesus; but He was manifested in the last days so that He might save us. And the Church, being spiritual, was manifested in the flesh of Christ."

St Irenaeus of Lyons, *Against Heresies* 3, 4, 1 (c. AD 180)
"When, therefore, we have such proofs, it is not necessary to seek among others the truth which is easily obtained from the Church. For the Apostles, like a rich man in a bank, deposited with her most copiously everything which pertains to the truth; and everyone whosoever wishes draws from her the drink of life. For she is the entrance to life, while all the rest are thieves and robbers. That is why it is surely necessary to avoid them, while cherishing with the utmost diligence the things pertaining to the Church, and to lay hold of the tradition of truth ... In the Church, God has placed apostles, prophets and doctors, and all the other means through which the Spirit works; in all of which none have any part who do not conform to the Church. On the contrary, they defraud themselves of life by their wicked opinion and most wretched behavior. For where the Church is, there is the Spirit of God; and where the Spirit of God, there the Church and every grace."

Clement of Alexandria, *Miscellanies* 7, 17, 107, 3 (post AD 202)
"From what has been said, then, it seems clear to me that the true Church, that which is really ancient, is one; and in it are enrolled those who, in accord with a design, are just ... We say, therefore, that in substance, in concept, in origin and in eminence, the ancient and Catholic Church is alone, gathering as it does into the unity of the one faith which results from the familiar covenants, – or rather, from the one covenant in different times, by the will of the one God and through the one Lord, – those already chosen, those predestined by God who knew before the foundation of the world that they would be just."

St Cyprian of Carthage, *Letter to all His People* 43, (40), 5 (AD 251)
"There is one God and one Christ, and one Church, and one Chair founded on Peter by the word of the Lord. It is not possible to set up another altar or for there to be another priesthood besides that one altar and that one priesthood. Whoever has gathered elsewhere is scattering."

Lactantius, *The Divine Institutions* 4, 30, 1 (inter AD 304-310)
"It is therefore, the Catholic Church alone which retains true worship. This is the fountain of truth; this, the domicile of faith; this, the temple of God. Whoever does not enter there or whoever does not go out from here, he is a stranger to the hope of life and salvation ... Because, however, all the various groups of heretics are confident that they are the Christians, and think that theirs is the Catholic Church, let it be known: that is the true Church, in which there is confession and penance, and which takes a salubrious care of the sins and wounds to which the weak flesh is subject."

The Roman Catechism (1566)

Pt. I, Ch. X: This Church was founded not by man, but by the immortal God Himself, who built her upon a most solid rock. *The Highest himself,* says the Prophet, *hath founded her.* Hence, she is called *the inheritance of God, the people of God.* The power which she possesses is not from man but from God.

Since this power, therefore, cannot be of human origin, divine faith can alone enable us to understand that the keys of the kingdom of heaven are deposited with the Church, that to her has been confided the power of remitting sins, of denouncing excommunication, and of consecrating the real body of Christ; and that her children have not here a permanent dwelling, but look for one above.

Catechism of the Catholic Church (1992)

No. 770: The Church is in history, but at the same time she transcends it. It is only "with the eyes of faith" that one can see her in her visible reality and at the same time in her spiritual reality as bearer of divine life.

No. 771: "The one mediator, Christ, established and ever sustains here on earth his holy Church, the community of faith, hope, and charity, as a visible organization through which he communicates truth and grace to all men." The Church is at the same time:
- a "society structured with hierarchical organs and the mystical body of Christ.
- the visible society and the spiritual community.
- the earthly Church and the Church endowed with heavenly riches."

These dimensions together constitute "one complex reality which comes from a human and a divine element":

> The Church is essentially both human and divine, visible but endowed with invisible realities, zealous in action and dedicated to contemplation, present in the world, but as a pilgrim, so constituted that in her the human is directed toward and subordinated to the divine, the visible to the invisible, action to contemplation, and this present world to that city yet to come, the object of our quest (SC 2).
>
> O humility! O humility! Both tabernacle of cedar and sanctuary of God; earthly dwelling and celestial palace; house of clay and royal hall; body of death and temple of light; and at last both object of scorn to the proud and bride of Christ! She is black but beautiful, O daughters of Jerusalem, for even if the labor and pain of her long exile may have discolored her, yet heaven's beauty has adorned her (St Bernard of Clairvaux, *In Cant. Sermo.* 27:14).

The Communion of Saints

"If one member suffers, all suffer together; if one member is honored, all rejoice together. Now you are the body of Christ and individually members of it" (1 Cor. 12:26-27).

The Communion of Saints is the union that exists between all the members of the Church on earth, in heaven, and in purgatory. Those members on earth comprise the *Church Militant*, those in heaven the *Church Triumphant*, those in purgatory the *Church Suffering*.

These three Churches, strictly speaking, form but one Church existing in three different states whose Head is Jesus Christ: "so we, though many, are one body in Christ, and individually members one of another" (Rom. 12:5). Every member has his own place and part to perform, not merely for his own benefit, but for the benefit of the whole Church: "And God has appointed in the church first apostles, second prophets, third teachers, then workers of miracles, then healers, helpers, administrators, speakers in various kinds of tongues" (1 Cor. 12:28). All the good works performed within the Church, and all the Church's spiritual treasures, are beneficial to all Her members.

The Church Militant is so-called as its members are still but wayfarers, working out their salvation in "fear and trembling" (Phil. 2:12), struggling against the "world, the flesh and the devil": "... he who endures to the end will be saved" (Mt 10:22). Only those who persevere can reach their goal; there can no reward for the weak and faint-hearted.

The members of the Church Militant are in communion with each other by:

I. Obedience to the same visible authority established by Christ Himself, that is, the rock of St Peter and his successor, the Pope of Rome.

II. Professing the same faith publicly as one body, such as the recitation of the Nicene Creed at weekly Mass. Through such, all the faithful

are "united in the same mind and the same judgment" (1 Cor. 1:10).
III. Assisting one another with their prayers and good works: "Bear one another's burdens, and so fulfil the law of Christ" (Gal. 6:2).

In other words, "it is a matter of communion with God through Jesus Christ, in the Holy Spirit. This communion is to be had in the Word of God and in the sacraments. Baptism is the door and the foundation of communion in the Church ... The communion of the eucharistic Body of Christ signifies and produces, that is, builds up, the intimate communion of all the faithful in the Body of Christ which is the Church" (Extraordinary Synod of Bishops, *Final Report*, 1985).

No member of the Church Militant, whatever his condition, stands alone: "If one member suffers, all suffer together; if one member is honored, all rejoice together. Now you are the body of Christ and individually members of it" (1 Cor. 12:26-27). The Church Militant is not a collection of individuals having their own "personal relationship with Christ" to the exclusion of all others. To commune with Christ requires a communion also with His Body, for one cannot claim to possess the Head to the exclusion of the Body: "and he has put all things under his feet and has made him the head over all things for the church which is his body, the fulness of him who fills all in all" (Eph. 1:22-23).

It is entirely appropriate to describe the Church in heaven as triumphant, for its members are those who have fought the "good fight" and have reached their port of destination. This triumph is reflected in the brightness of the Just in heaven: "There is one glory of the sun, and another glory of the moon, and another glory of the stars; for star differs from star in glory" (1 Cor. 15:41). Each member of the Church Triumphant will be crowned in reward for his or her victory: "I have fought the good fight, I have finished the race, I have kept the faith. Henceforth there is laid up for me the crown of righteousness, which the Lord, the righteous judge, will award to me on that Day" (2 Tim. 4:7). The devil and his cohorts have been frustrated in their efforts to destroy these souls, and now they reign with their heavenly Lord and Master as their eternal reward.

As we are united with Christ our Head in heaven, so are we united with His members triumphantly reigning with Him. Death in no way impedes our union with the Church Triumphant any more than it impedes our union with Christ Himself. Together, the Church Militant and the Church Triumphant unceasingly bless and praise God. Furthermore, we can ask the Saints in heaven to intercede on our behalf to obtain God's blessings and favors. When those in heaven see that one on earth has turned away from evil to do good they immediately express their joy: "I tell you, there is joy before the angels of God over one sinner who repents" (Lk 15:10). The Saints enjoy the same Beatific Vision as the angels and hence are also witnesses to the struggles of the saints on earth: "Therefore, since we are surrounded by so great a cloud of witnesses, let us also lay aside every weight, and sin which clings so closely" (Heb. 12:1).

The Church Suffering, though its members have also been found worthy to share in eternal life, are obliged to undergo a period of purgation, or cleansing, for their unforgiven venial sins and/or lack of penance for mortal sin duly forgiven. This purgation, though temporary, is effected by purifying fires that burn at the soul: "If any man's work is burned up, he will suffer loss, though he himself will be saved, but only as through fire" (1 Cor. 3:15). From the writings of Mystics, Doctors and Saints, we know that these fires burn with a degree of intensity not found on earth, inflicting the acutest pain. Hence, the appropriateness of the term "suffering."

Our communion with the Church Suffering is effected by praying for the souls in purgatory, by assisting them through good works and penances, especially the Holy Sacrifice of the Mass: "But if he was looking to the splendid reward that is laid up for those who fall asleep in godliness, it was a holy and pious thought. Therefore he made atonement for the dead, that they might be delivered from their sin" (2 Macc. 12:45). Through such acts of charity, the Holy Souls earn an abatement of their sufferings; and they, in turn, will in gratitude pray for us.

The Fathers

Origen, *On Prayer* 11, 2 (post AD 231)
"Now the one great virtue according to the Word of God is love of one's neighbor. We must believe that the saints who have died possess this love in a far higher degree towards the ones engaged in the combat of life than those who are still subject to human weakness and involved in the

combat along with their weaker brethren. The words 'If one member suffer anything, all the members suffer with it, or if one member glory, all the members rejoice with it' are not confined to those on earth who love their brethren. For the words apply just as much to the love of those who have left this present life ... 'the solicitude for all the churches. Who is weak, and I am not weak? Who is scandalized and I am not inflamed?'"

St Jerome, *Against Vigilantius* 6 (AD 406)
"You say in your book that while we live we are able to pray for each other, but afterwards when we have died, the prayer of no person for another can be heard; and this is especially clear since the martyrs, though they cry vengeance for their own blood, have never been able to obtain their request. But if the Apostles and martyrs while still in the body can pray for others, at a time when they ought still to be solicitous about themselves, how much more will they do so after their crowns, victories, and triumphs."

St Augustine of Hippo, *The Care of the Dead* 15, 18 (AD 421)
"The spirits of the dead are able to know some things which happen here, which it is necessary for them to know. And those for whom it is necessary that something be known, not only the present or the past but even the future,—they know these things by the revealing Spirit of God, just as not all men but the Prophets, while they lived, knew not all things but those which the providence of God judged ought to be revealed to them."

St Augustine of Hippo, *The City of God* Bk. 20, Ch. 9 (ante AD 427)
"Neither are the souls of the pious dead separated from the Church which even now is the Kingdom of Christ. Otherwise there would be no remembrance of them at the altar of God in the communication of the Body of Christ."

The Roman Catechism (1566)

Pt. I, Ch. X: For the unity of the Spirit, by which she is governed, brings it about that whatsoever has been given to the Church is held as a common possession by all her members ... The same may be observed in the Church. She is composed of various members; that is, of different nations, of Jews, Gentiles, freemen and slaves, of rich and poor; when they have been baptized, they constitute one body with Christ, of which He is the Head.

Catechism of the Catholic Church (1992)

No. 954: *The three states of the Church.* "When the Lord comes in glory, and all his angels with him, death will be no more and all things will be subject to him. But at the present time some of his disciples are pilgrims on earth. Others have died and are being purified, while still others are in glory, contemplating 'in full light, God himself triune and one, exactly as he is'":

> All of us, however, in varying degrees and in different ways share in the same charity towards God and our neighbors, and we all sing the one hymn of glory to our God. All, indeed, who are of Christ and who have his Spirit form one Church and in Christ cleave together.

No. 957: *Communion with the saints.* "It is not merely by the title of example that we cherish the memory of those in heaven; we seek, rather, that by this devotion to the exercise of fraternal charity the union of the whole Church in the Spirit may be strengthened. Exactly as Christian communion among our fellow pilgrims brings us closer to Christ, so our communion with the saints joins us to Christ, from which as from its fountain and head issues all grace, and the life of the People of God itself":

> We worship Christ as God's Son; we love the martyrs as the Lord's disciples and imitators, and rightly so because of their matchless devotion towards their king and master. May we also be their companions and fellow disciples! (*Mart. Polycarpi*, 17).

No. 958: *Communion with the dead.* In full consciousness of this communion of the whole Mystical Body of Jesus Christ, the Church in its pilgrim members, from the very earliest days of the Christian religion, has honored with great respect the memory of the dead; and because 'it is a holy and wholesome thought to pray for the dead that they may be loosed from their sins' (2 Macc. 12, 45) she offers her suffrages for them. Our prayer for them is capable not only of helping them, but also of making their intercession for us effective.

The Forgiveness of Sins

"Blessed be the God and Father of our Lord Jesus Christ ... In him we have redemption through his blood, the forgiveness of our trespasses, according to the riches of his grace" (Eph. 1:3; 7).

"All authority", said Christ to His Apostles, "in heaven and on earth has been given to me" (Mt 28:18). Included in this was the power to forgive sins. The following incident in the Gospels testifies to Christ's power to forgive sins:

"Jesus saw their faith he said to the paralytic, 'Take heart, my son; your sins are forgiven.' And behold, some of the scribes said to themselves, 'This man is blaspheming.' But Jesus, knowing their thoughts, said, 'Why do you think evil in your hearts? For which is easier, to say, Your sins are forgiven, or to say, Rise and walk? But that you may know that the Son of man has authority on earth to forgive sins – he then said to the paralytic –Rise, take up your bed and go home.' And he rose and went home" (Mt 9:2-7).

It was this same spiritual power to forgive sins that Our Lord communicated to His Apostles and their successors after His resurrection:

"As the Father has sent me, even so I send you ... Receive the Holy Spirit. If you forgive the sins of any, they are forgiven; if you retain the sins of any, they are retained" (Jn 20:21-23).

In this verse we see that Christ bestowed upon His Apostles the following: (i) mission (*"As the Father has sent me, even so I send you ..."*); (ii) power (*"Receive the Holy Spirit"*), and (iii) judgment as to when and how to exercise this power (*"If you forgive ...; if you retain"*). This verse cannot be explained away by claiming that the Apostles were simply authorized to go out and preach forgiveness according to the following injunction: "that repentance and forgiveness of sins should be preached in his name to all nations" (Lk 24:47). If such were the case Jn 20:21-23 would be utterly devoid of purpose.

The power to forgive sins was the first charism Christ bestowed upon the Apostles after His resurrection. In claiming that Her priests have the power to forgive sins, the Catholic Church is criticized and accused of carrying out a function that is proper to God alone. It is the same accusation Christ Himself had to endure: "This man is blaspheming" (Mt 9:3). Yet, Christ established the Church to continue His work of salvation in the world after His ascension into heaven. Whatever Christ as Head possesses by way of power and authority is properly possessed by His Body also, that is, the Church. In forgiving sins, priests and bishops act as Christ's ministers and instruments; the fact that they may be sinners themselves does not inhibit the exercise or effectiveness of this power.

The main ways by which the power to forgive sins is exercised in the Church are through the sacraments of Baptism and Penance. It is through Baptism that the merits of Christ's redemption are applied to us for the remission of original sin inherited from Adam: "Truly, truly, I say to you, unless one is born of water and the Spirit, he cannot enter the kingdom of God" (Jn 3:5). Penance forgives all actual sin committed after Baptism.

Actual sin can be either venial or mortal. Venial sin is a transgression of the law of God in a slight matter, or in a grave matter when, at the time, either our understanding does not comprehend the gravity of the evil presented to it, or there is wanting full consent of the will. Mortal sin is a grievous offense that brings death to the soul and loss of God's friendship. For mortal sin to be committed there must be:

(i) Grave matter.
(ii) Full knowledge of the gravity of the act being committed.
(iii) Full consent of the will to the commission of the act.

There are some who claim that the distinction made by the Church between venial and mortal sin is artificial, and that all sin is equally bad ("sin is sin"). The difference in degrees of sin is clearly indicated by the following verses: "Why do you see the speck that is in your brother's eye, but do not notice the log that is in your own eye?" (Mt 7:3); "... therefore he who delivered me to you has the greater sin" (Jn 19:11); finally, "If any one sees his brother committing what is not a mortal sin, he will ask, and God will give him life for those whose sin is not mortal. There is sin which is mortal; I do not say that one is to pray for that. All wrongdoing is sin, but there is sin which is not mortal" (Jn 5:16-17).

The Fathers

St Ignatius of Antioch, *Letter to the Philadelphians* 8, 1 (c. AD 110)
"The Lord, however, forgives all who repent, if their repentance leads to the unity of God and to the council of the bishop. I have faith in the grace of Jesus Christ; and He will remove from you every chain."

Firmilian of Caesarea, *Letter to Cyprian* 75, 16 (c. AD 268)
"'Receive the Holy Spirit: if you forgive any man his sins, they shall be forgiven; and if you retain any man's sins, they shall be retained.' Therefore, the power of forgiving sins was given to the Apostles and to the Churches which these men, sent by Christ, established; and to the bishops who succeeded them by being ordained in their place."

Lactantius, *The Divine Institutions* 4, 30, 1 (inter AD 304-310)
"Let it be known: that is the true Church, in which there is confession and penance, and which takes a salubrious care of the sins and wounds to which the weak flesh is subject."

St Hilary of Poitiers, *Commentary on the Gospel of Matthew* 18, 8 (c. AD 353-355)
"In our present condition we are all subdued by the terror of that greatest dread. And now, out in front of that terror, He sets the irrevocable apostolic judgment, however severe, so that those whom they shall bind on earth, that is, whomsoever they leave bound in the knots of their sins; and those whom they loose, which is to say, those who by their confession receive grace unto salvation:—these, in accord with the apostolic sentence, are bound or loosed also in heaven."

St Pacian of Barcelona, *Letters to Sympronian* 1, 6 (inter AD 375-392)
"God never threatens the repentant, rather He pardons the penitent. You will say that it is God alone who can do this. True enough, but it is likewise true that He does it through his priests, who exercise His power."

The Roman Catechism (1566)

Pt. I, Ch. XI: As, therefore, He became man, in order to bestow on man this forgiveness of sins, He communicated this power to Bishops and priests in the Church, previous to His Ascension into heaven, where He sits forever at the right hand of God. Christ, however, as we have already said, remits sin by virtue of His own authority; all others, by virtue of His authority delegated to them as His ministers.

Catechism of the Catholic Church (1992)

No. 976: The Apostles' Creed associates faith in the forgiveness of sins not only with faith in the Holy Spirit, but also with faith in the Church and in the communion of saints. It was when he gave the Holy Spirit to his apostles that the risen Christ conferred on them his own divine power to forgive sins: "Receive the Holy Spirit. If you forgive the sins of any, they are forgiven; if you retain the sins of any, they are retained."

No. 981: After his Resurrection, Christ sent his apostles "so that repentance and forgiveness of sins should be preached in his name to all nations." The apostles and their successors carry out this "ministry of reconciliation," not only by announcing to men God's forgiveness merited for us by Christ, and calling them to conversion and faith; but also by communicating to them the forgiveness of sins in Baptism, and reconciling them with God and with the Church through the power of the keys, received from Christ:

> [The Church] has received the keys of the Kingdom of heaven so that, in her, sins may be forgiven through Christ's blood and the Holy Spirit's action. In this Church, the soul dead through sin

comes back to life in order to live with Christ, whose grace has saved us (St Augustine, *Sermo* 214,11).

No. 982: There is no offense, however serious, that the Church cannot forgive. "There is no one, however wicked and guilty, who may not confidently hope for forgiveness, provided his repentance is honest." Christ who died for all men desires that in his Church the gates of forgiveness should always be open to anyone who turns away from sin.

The Resurrection of the Body

"For I know that my Redeemer lives, and at last he will stand upon the earth; and after my skin has been thus destroyed, then from my flesh I shall see God, whom I shall see on my side, and my eyes shall behold, and not another. My heart faints within me!" (Job 19:25-27).

According to God's original plan for humanity, Adam and Eve and their descendants were to live in Paradise on earth until they attained a certain level of grace through a life of meritorious acts. Thereupon, each person would be assumed body and soul into heavenly glory without having to endure sickness, pain, suffering or death. This was the proper end for humanity by virtue of the preternatural gifts of impassibility and immortality, gifts that our original parents forfeited by their rebellion against God. Hence, it is now the lot of all men to die, a decree issued against all the children of Adam: "Therefore as sin came into the world through one man and death through sin, and so death spread to all men because all men sinned" (Rom. 5:12).

At death, the human soul departs from its mortal body and immediately comes before the judgment-seat of God; the body returns to the earth from whence it came: "the dust returns to the earth as it was, and the spirit returns to God who gave it" (Eccl. 12:7). This judgment the Church calls the *particular* judgment for it is the private judgment of each individual before Christ in contrast to the *general* judgment when all of humanity will be publicly gathered together before Christ at the end of the world: "Before him will be gathered all the nations, and he will separate them one from another ... And they will go away into eternal punishment, but the righteous into eternal life" (Mt 25:32-46).

The bodies of the dead will remain in the earth until the Last Day, or Day of Judgment, when Jesus Christ will descend from heaven to call all back to life. At that instant, all departed souls will be reunited with their bodies: "For the trumpet will sound, and the dead will be raised imperishable" (1 Cor. 15:52). Those who are alive at this time will have their bodies transformed instantly: "we shall all be changed, in a moment, in the twinkling of an eye" (1 Cor. 15:51-52).

Every soul shall be re-united with the same body it possessed during life, so that, as the body shared in its good or evil, so may it share in its glory or condemnation: "those who have done good, to the resurrection of life, and those who have done evil, to the resurrection of judgment" (Jn 5:29); "For we must all appear before the judgment seat of Christ, so that each one may receive good or evil, according to what he has done in the body" (2 Cor. 5:10).

Through the resurrection of the body, Christ's victory over death is complete: "Death is swallowed up in victory. O death, where is thy victory? O death, where is thy sting?" (1 Cor. 15:54-55).

St Paul tells us that as the sun is brighter than the moon, and one star brighter than another, so shall it be with the merits of the risen at the Resurrection: "There are celestial bodies and there are terrestrial bodies; but the glory of the celestial is one, and the glory of the terrestrial is another. There is one glory of the sun, and another glory of the moon, and another glory of the stars; for star differs from star in glory" (1 Cor. 15:40-41).

The bodies of the Just after the Resurrection shall possess four principal qualities:

(i) *Impassibility*: this will render them incapable of pain or suffering: "he will wipe away every tear from their eyes, and death shall be no more, neither shall there be mourning nor crying nor pain any more" (Rev. 21:4).
(ii) *Brightness*: this will render them as glorious as the sun: "... Then the righteous will shine like the sun in the kingdom of their Father" (Mt 13:43).
(iii) *Agility*: this will give them the ability, as quick as thought, to move from one end of creation to another: "It is sown in dishonor, it is raised in glory" (1 Cor. 15:43).
(iv) *Subtility*: this will make them completely subject to the soul and give them spirit-like qualities: "It is sown a physical body, it is raised a spiritual body" (1 Cor. 15:44).

The opposite of these gifts will be the fate of the reprobate, as just punishment for their lives of sin and self-indulgence:

(i) *Darkness*: Their bodies will be dark and "... they will look aghast at one another; their faces will be aflame" (Is. 13:8).
(ii) *Passibility*: Their bodies will suffer endless pain and torment, burning forever in the fire without being consumed: "for their worm shall not die, their fire shall not be quenched" (Is. 66:24; Mk 9:48).
(iii) *Heaviness*: Their bodies will be weighed down and sluggish: "to bind their kings with chains and their nobles with fetters of iron" (Ps. 149:8).
(iv) *Carnality*: Their souls will be subject and enslaved to their bodies: "... for whatever a man sows, that he will also reap. For he who sows to his own flesh will from the flesh reap corruption" (Gal. 6:7-8).

The thought of the future resurrection should be our great incentive to yield our bodies "to righteousness for sanctification" (Rom. 6:19). It is our great hope, the crown of our faith: "But if there is no resurrection of the dead, then Christ has not been raised; if Christ has not been raised, then our preaching is in vain and your faith is in vain" (1 Cor. 15:13-14).

The Fathers

The Didache 16, 3 (inter AD 90-150)
"And then will appear the signs of the truth. First, the sign spread out in the heavens; second, the sign of the sound of the trumpet; the third, the resurrection of the dead. Not the resurrection of all men, but as it was said: 'The Lord will come, and all His saints with Him.' Then the world will see the Lord coming on the clouds of heaven."

St Justin Martyr, *The Resurrection* 8 (ante AD 160)
"Indeed, God calls even the body to resurrection, and promises it everlasting life. When He promises to save the man, He thereby makes His promise to the flesh: for what is man but a rational living being composed of soul and body?"

Athenagoras of Athens, *The Resurrection of the Dead* **12 (c. AD 177-180)**
"And the body is moved to what is proper to it in accord with its nature, and undergoes the changes allotted to it; and among the other changes of age, appearance and size, is the resurrection. For the resurrection is a species of change, the last of all, and a change for the better in those things which remain at that time."

Tertullian, *The Resurrection of the Dead* **63, 1 (inter AD 208-212)**
"Therefore, the flesh shall rise again: certainly of every man, certainly the same flesh, and certainly in its entirety. Whatever it is, it is in safe keeping with God through that most faithful Agent between God and man, Jesus Christ, who shall reconcile both God to man and man to God, the spirit to the flesh and the flesh to the spirit."

St Hippolytus of Rome, *Against the Greeks* **2 (ante AD 225)**
"Not in vain, then, do we believe in the resurrection of the body. Moreover, while it is dissolved at its proper time because of the transgression which took place in the beginning, and is committed to the earth as to a furnace, to be reshaped again, not in its present corruption, but pure and no longer corruptible, so also to every body its own soul will be returned; and the soul, being clothed with it again, will not be grieved but will rejoice with it, the pure abiding in the pure. Just as the soul now abides with the body in this world in righteousness, and finds the body in no way uncooperative, so to, in all joy it will receive the body again."

St Cyril of Jerusalem, *Catechetical Lectures* **18, 1 (c. AD 350)**
"The root of every good work is the hope of the resurrection; for the expectation of a reward nerves the soul to good work. Every laborer is prepared to endure the toils if he looks forward to the reward of these toils. But they who labor without reward – their soul is exhausted with their body ... He that believes his body will remain for the resurrection is careful of his garment and does not soil it in fornication, or abuses his own body as if it belonged to another. A great precept and teaching of the Holy Catholic Church, therefore, is belief in the resurrection of the dead – great and most necessary, but contradicted by many..."

The Roman Catechism (1566)

Pt. I, Ch. XII: Not only will the body rise, but whatever belongs to the reality of its nature, and adorns and ornaments man will be restored. For this we have the admirable words of St Augustine: *There shall then be no deformity of body; if some have been overburdened with flesh, they shall not resume its entire weight. All that exceeds the proper proportion shall be deemed superfluous. On the other hand, should the body be wasted by disease or old age, or be emaciated from any other cause, it shall be repaired by the divine power of Christ, who will not only restore the body unto us, but will repair whatever it shall have lost through the wretchedness of this life.* In another place he says: *Man shall not resume his former hair, but shall be adorned with such as will become him, according to the words: "The very hairs of your head are all numbered."* God will restore them according to His wisdom.

Catechism of the Catholic Church (1992)

No. 989: We firmly believe, and hence we hope that, just as Christ is truly risen from the dead and lives forever, so after death the righteous will live forever with the risen Christ and he will raise them up on the last day. Our resurrection, like his own, will be the work of the Most Holy Trinity:

> If the Spirit of him who raised Jesus from the dead dwells in you, he who raised Christ Jesus from the dead will give life to your mortal bodies also through his Spirit who dwells in you (Rom. 8, 11).

No. 994: But there is more. Jesus links faith in the resurrection to his own person: "I am the Resurrection and the life." It is Jesus himself who on the last day will raise up those who have believed in him, who have eaten his body and drunk his blood. Already now in this present life he gives a sign and pledge of this by restoring some of the dead to life, announcing thereby his own Resurrection, though it was to be of another order. He speaks of this unique event as the "sign of Jonah," the sign of the temple: he announces that he will be put to death but rise thereafter on the third day.

No. 996: From the beginning, Christian faith in the resurrection has met with incomprehension and opposition. "On no point does the Christian faith encounter more opposition than on the resurrection of the body" (St Augustine). It is very commonly accepted that the life of the human person continues in a spiritual fashion after death. But how can we believe that this body, so clearly mortal, could rise to everlasting life?

No. 1000: This "how" exceeds our imagination and understanding; it is accessible only to faith. Yet our participation in the Eucharist already gives us a foretaste of Christ's transfiguration of our bodies:

> Just as bread that comes from the earth, after God's blessing has been invoked upon it, is no longer ordinary bread, but Eucharist, formed of two things, the one earthly and the other heavenly: so too our bodies, which partake of the Eucharist, are no longer corruptible, but possess the hope of resurrection (St Irenaeus, *Against Heresies* 4, 18, 4-5).

And Life Everlasting.
Amen.

"What no eye has seen, nor ear heard, nor the heart of man conceived, what God has prepared for those who love him" (1 Cor. 2:9).

After this life there is one of two eternities that awaits each individual: an eternity of happiness in heaven as reward for remaining faithful to God, or an eternity of misery in hell for having rejected him.

The joy of heaven, once obtained, can never be lost. It consists of the Beatific Vision, that is, in seeing, possessing and loving God as He is for all eternity: "For now we see in a mirror dimly, but then face to face" (1 Cor. 13:12). All the sufferings and ills of this life shall pass away, replaced by eternal happiness in the company of the angelic hosts and Saints: "For the Lamb in the midst of the throne will be their shepherd, and he will guide them to springs of living water; and God will wipe away every tear from their eyes" (Rev. 7:17).

Not all, however, will be equally happy. The happiness and glory of each will be dependent on their merits: "each shall receive his wages according to his labor" (1 Cor. 3:8); "There is one glory of the sun, and another glory of the moon, and another glory of the stars; for star differs from star in glory" (1 Cor. 15:41). Nevertheless, despite this inequality all will be fully content and happy, rejoicing in each other's glory, and blessing God's mercy and justice.

Three particular categories of Saints shall receive a distinct glory:

(i) *The Martyrs*: those who laid down their lives for Christ will be marked with a special glory on account of their sufferings: "But rejoice in so far as you share Christ's sufferings, that you may also rejoice and be glad when his glory is revealed" (1 Pet. 4:13).
(ii) *The Virgins*: those who "made themselves eunuchs for the sake of the kingdom of heaven" (Mt 19:12) will be clothed in white garments and will "and they sing a new song before the throne and before the four living creatures and before the elders" (Rev. 14:3-4).

(iii) *The Doctors of the Church*: the great teachers, apologists, Fathers, Scholastics, etc., who taught and defended the Catholic Faith will shine with a special brightness: "And those who are wise shall shine like the brightness of the firmament; and those who turn many to righteousness, like the stars for ever and ever" (Dan. 12:3).

For those who refused to serve God and rejected His graces the following sentence shall be theirs: "Depart from me, you cursed, into the eternal fire prepared for the devil and his angels" (Mt 25:41). Those condemned to hell shall endure two particular torments:

(i) *The pain of loss*: arises from the regret at having irrevocably lost God forever through their own fault: "where their worm does not die" (Mk 9:48) – the gnawing of conscience forever rebuking them for their folly.
(ii) *The pain of sense*: caused by the fires of hell, forever burning yet never consuming: "Father Abraham, have mercy upon me, and send Lazarus to dip the end of his finger in water and cool my tongue; for I am in anguish in this flame" (Lk 16:24).

The damned will suffer in proportion to their sins and to the rejection of the graces offered them: "he will repay every man for what he has done" (Mt 16:27). The sufferings of hell are unimaginable, though the following graphic account given by Sister Lucia (one of the three child seers of Fatima) affords some idea of their extent:

> "As she (Our Lady) said these last words she once again opened her hands as she had done in the two previous months. The radiant light seemed to penetrate the earth, and we saw, as it were, a great sea of fire; submerged in that fire were demons and souls in human shapes who resembled red-hot, black and bronze-colored embers that floated about in the blaze, borne by the flames that issued from them with clouds of smoke, falling everywhere like the showering sparks of great blazes - with neither weight or equilibrium - amidst shrieks and groans

of sorrow and despair that horrified us and made us shudder with fear."[1]

The thought of hell should always be a matter for meditation and serve as a deterrence to sin. Yet, Scripture sadly indicates that not all will avail themselves of this opportunity: "Enter by the narrow gate; for the gate is wide and the way is easy, that leads to destruction, and those who enter by it are many. For the gate is narrow and the way is hard, that leads to life, and those who find it are few" (Mt 7:13-14).

Our Creed concludes with the word *Amen*, the Hebrew word for "So be it", by which we express our belief in all the Articles of the Creed, and our resolution to remain faithful in them until the end.

The Fathers

Tertullian, *Apology* 18, 3 (AD 197)
"After the present age is ended He will judge His worshippers for a reward of eternal life, and the godless for a fire equally perpetual and unending. All who have died since the beginning of time will be raised up again and shaped again and remanded to whichever destiny they deserve."

St Cyprian of Carthage, *Letter to the People of Thibar* 58, 10 (AD 253)
"Oh, what a day that will be, and how great when it comes, dearest brethren! when the Lord begins to survey His people and to recognize by examining with divine knowledge the merits of each individual! to cast into hell evildoers, and to condemn our persecutors to the eternal fire and punishing flame! and indeed, to present to us the reward of faith and devotion! What will be that glory, and how great the joy of being admitted to the sight of God! to be so honored as to receive the joy of eternal light and salvation in the presence of Christ the Lord, your God!"

---

[1] The Third Apparition of Our Lady of Fatima, 13 July, 1917 (The First Part of the Secret: The Vision of Hell).

Aphraates the Persian Sage, *Treatises* **20, 12 (inter AD 336-345)**
"And Abraham said to the rich man, 'There is a great abyss separating us from you; they cannot come from you to us, nor from us to you.' This shows that after death and resurrection there will be no repentance. Neither can the wicked repent and enter the kingdom, nor can the righteous any longer sin and go to perdition. This is the great abyss."

St Augustine of Hippo, *Enchiridion of Faith, Hope & Love* **29, 111 (AD 421)**
"After the resurrection, however, when the universal and final judgment has been made, two cities will have their boundaries: one, of course, of Christ, and the other of the devil; one of the good, the other of the wicked; yet both made up of angels and of men. For the one group there will be no will to sin, and for the other, no power to do so; nor will there be any possibility of dying. The former will be living truly and happily in eternal life; the latter will be enduring unhappily in eternal death without the power to die; for both shall be without end. Among the former one man will be pre-eminent in happiness than another, and among the latter the abiding misery of one man will be more tolerable than that of another."

The Roman Catechism (1566)

Pt. I, Ch. XIII: Solid happiness, which we may designate by the common appellation, *essential*, consists in the vision of God, and the enjoyment of His beauty who is the source and principle of all goodness and perfection. *This*, says Christ our Lord, *is eternal life; that they may know thee, the only true God, and Jesus Christ, whom thou hast sent.* These words St John seems to interpret when he says: *Dearly beloved, we are now the sons of God; and it hath not yet appeared what we shall be. We know that when he shall appear, we shall be like to him: because we shall see him as he is.* He shows, then, that beatitude consists of two things: that we shall behold God such as He is in His own nature and substance; and that we ourselves shall become, as it were, gods.

And Life Everlasting. Amen.

Catechism of the Catholic Church (1992)

No. 1024: This perfect life with the Most Holy Trinity--this consummation of life with the Trinity, with the Virgin Mary, the angels and all the blessed - is called "heaven." Heaven is the ultimate end and fulfillment of the deepest human longings, the state of supreme, definitive happiness.

No. 1035: The teaching of the Church affirms the existence of hell and its eternity. Immediately after death the souls of those who die in a state of mortal sin descend into hell, where they suffer the punishments of hell, "eternal fire." The chief punishment of hell is eternal separation from God, in whom alone man can possess the life and happiness for which he was created and for which he longs.

No. 1042: At the end of time, the Kingdom of God will come in its fullness. After the universal judgment, the righteous will reign forever with Christ, glorified in body and soul. The universe itself will be renewed:

> The Church ... will receive her perfection only in the glory of heaven, when will come the time of the renewal of all things. At that time, together with the human race, the universe itself, which is so closely related to man and which attains its destiny through him, will be perfectly re-established in Christ.

Appendix

CREEDS AND PROFESSIONS OF FAITH

THE APOSTLES' CREED
(c. 3rd century AD)

I believe in God, the Father Almighty, Creator of heaven and earth; and in Jesus Christ, His only Son, Our Lord; Who was conceived by the Holy Spirit, born of the Virgin Mary, suffered under Pontius Pilate, was crucified, died, and was buried. He descended into hell; the third day He rose again from the dead; He ascended into heaven, is seated at the right hand of God the Father Almighty; from thence He shall come to judge the living and the dead. I believe in the Holy Spirit, the Holy Catholic Church, the communion of saints, the forgiveness of sins, the resurrection of the flesh, and life everlasting. Amen.

THE DER-BALIZEH PAPYRUS
(c. late 2nd century AD)

I believe in God, the Father almighty, and in His only-begotten Son, Jesus Christ, and in the Holy Spirit, and in the resurrection of the flesh, and in the Holy Catholic Church.

THE 'CREED' OF ST IRENAEUS OF LYONS
(*Against Heresies* 1, 10, 1)
(c. AD 180)

For the Church, although dispersed throughout the whole world even to the ends of the earth, has received from the Apostles and from their disciples the faith in one God, Father Almighty, the Creator of heaven and earth and sea and all that is in them; and in one Jesus Christ, the Son of God who became flesh for our salvation; and in the Holy Spirit, who announced through the prophets the dispensations and the comings, and the birth from a Virgin, and the passion, and the resurrection from the dead, and the bodily ascension into heaven in the glory of the Father to re-establish all things; and the raising up again of all flesh of all humanity, in order that to Jesus Christ our Lord and God and Savior and King, in accord with the approval of the invisible Father, every knee shall bend of those in heaven and on earth and under the earth, and that every tongue shall confess Him, and that He may make just judgment of them all; and that He may send the spiritual forces of wickedness and the angels who transgressed and became apostates, and the impious, unjust, lawless and blasphemous amongst men, into everlasting fire; and that He may grant life, immortality, and surround with eternal glory the just and the holy, and those who have kept His commands and who have persevered in His love, either from the beginning or from their repentance.

THE 'CREED' OF TERTULLIAN
(*Against Praxeas* 2, 1)
(inter AD 213-220)

We do indeed believe that there is only one God; but we believe that under this dispensation ... there is also a Son of this one only God, His Word, who proceeded from Him and through whom all things were made and without whom nothing was made. We believe that He was sent by the Father into a Virgin and was born of her, God and man, Son of man and Son of God, and was called by the name Jesus Christ. We believe that He suffered and that, in accord with the Scriptures, He died and was buried; and that He was raised again by the Father to resume His place in heaven, sitting at the right of the Father; and that He will come to judge the living and the dead. We believe that He sent down from the Father, in accord with His own promise, the Holy Spirit, the Paraclete, the Sanctifier of the faith of those who believe in the Father and in the Son and in the Holy Spirit ... That this rule of faith has been current since the beginning of the Gospel, before even the earlier heretics, - much more then, before Praxeas, who was but of yesterday ...

Appendix

THE APOSTOLIC TRADITION OF ST HIPPOLYTUS
(c. AD 216)

Do you believe in God, the Father almighty?
Do you believe in Jesus Christ, the Son of God, who was born of the Virgin Mary by the Holy Spirit, has been crucified under Pontius Pilate, died [and was buried], who, on the third day
rose again, alive, from the dead, ascended into heaven and took His seat at the right hand of the Father, and shall come to judge the living and the dead?
Do you believe in the Holy Church and the resurrection of the body in the Holy Spirit?

THE CREED OF EUSEBIUS
(AD 325)

We believe in one God, the Father almighty, the maker of all things visible and invisible. And in one Lord Jesus Christ, the Word of God, God from God, light from light, Life from Life, the only-begotten Son, first born of all creation, begotten from the Father before all ages, through whom all things were made. For our salvation He became flesh and lived as a man, He suffered and rose again on the third day and ascended to the Father. He shall come again in glory to judge the living and the dead. We believe also in one Holy Spirit.

CREED OF THE FIRST GENERAL
COUNCIL OF NICAEA (AD 325)

We believe in one God, the Father almighty, maker of all things, visible and invisible. And in one Lord Jesus Christ, the Son of God, the only-begotten generated from the Father, that is, from the being of the Father, God from God, Light from Light, true God from true God, begotten, not made, consubstantial (*homo-ousios*) with the Father, through whom all things were made, those in heaven and those on earth. For us men and for our salvation He came down, and became flesh, was made man, suffered, and rose again on the third day. He ascended to the heavens and shall come again to judge the living and the dead. And in the Holy Spirit.

As for those who say: "There was a time when He was not" and "Before being begotten He was not", and who declare that He was made from nothing, or that the Son of God is from a different substance or being, that is, created or subject to change and alteration, such persons the Catholic Church condemns.

THE CREED OF ST CYRIL OF JERUSALEM
(c. AD 348)

We believe in one God, the Father almighty, maker of heaven and earth, of all things visible and invisible. And in one Lord Jesus Christ, the only-begotten Son of God, generated from the Father, true God before all the ages, through whom all things were made. He [came down, became flesh and] was made man, was crucified [and buried]. He rose again [from the dead] on the third day, and ascended to the heavens, and took His seat at the right hand of the Father. He shall come in glory to judge the living and the dead; to His Kingdom there will be no end. And in one Holy Spirit, the Paraclete, who has spoken in the prophets, and in one baptism of conversion for the forgiveness of sins, and in one Holy and Catholic Church, and in the resurrection of the body, and the life everlasting.

THE CREED OF ST EPIPHANIUS OF SALAMIS
(AD 374)

We believe in one God, the Father almighty, maker of heaven and earth, of all things visible and invisible. And in one Lord Jesus Christ, the only-begotten Son of God, generated from the Father before all ages, that is, from the being of the Father, Light from Light, true God from true God, begotten, not made, consubstantial (*homo-ousios*) with the Father, through whom all things were made, those in the heavens and those on earth. For us men and for our salvation He came down from the heavens, and became flesh from the Holy Spirit and the Virgin Mary, and was made man. For our sake too He was crucified under Pontius Pilate, suffered and was buried. On the third day He rose again according to the Scriptures. He ascended to the heavens and is seated at the right hand of the Father. He shall come again in glory to judge the living and the dead; to His Kingdom there will be no end. And in the

Holy Spirit, the Lord and Giver of life, who proceeds from the Father, who together with the Father and the Son is worshipped and glorified, who has spoken through the prophets. (And) in one Holy, Catholic and Apostolic Church. We acknowledge one baptism for the forgiveness of sins. We expect the resurrection of the dead and the life of the world to come. Amen.

As for those who say: "There was a time when He was not," and "Before being begotten He was not," or who declare that He was made from nothing, or that the Son of God is from a different substance or being, or subject to change and alteration, such persons the Catholic and apostolic Church condemns.

THE CREED OF THE FIRST GENERAL COUNCIL OF CONSTANTINOPLE (AD 381)

We believe in one God, the Father almighty, maker of heaven and earth, of all things visible and invisible. And in one Lord Jesus Christ, the only-begotten Son of God, generated from the Father before all ages, Light from Light, true God from true God, begotten, not made, consubstantial (*homo-ousios*) with the Father, through whom all things were made. For us men and for our salvation He came down from the heavens, and became flesh from the Holy Spirit and the Virgin Mary and was made man. For our sake too He was crucified under Pontius Pilate, suffered and was buried. On the third day He rose again according to the Scriptures, He ascended to the heavens and is seated at the right hand of the Father. He shall come again in glory to judge the living and the dead; to His Kingdom there will be no end. And in the Holy Spirit, the Lord and Giver of life, who proceeds from the Father, who together with the Father and the Son is worshipped and glorified, who has spoken through the prophets. (And) in one Holy Catholic and Apostolic Church. We acknowledge one baptism for the forgiveness of sins. We expect the resurrection of the dead and the life of the world to come. Amen.

THE CREED OF ST AMBROSE OF MILAN
(pre AD 397)

I believe in God, the Father almighty, and in Jesus Christ, His only Son, our Lord, who was born of the Virgin Mary by the Holy Spirit, who suffered under Pontius Pilate, died and was buried. On the third day He rose again from the dead. He ascended into heaven, and is seated at the right hand of the Father, wherefrom He shall come to judge the living and the dead. And in the Holy Spirit, the Holy Church, the forgiveness of sins and the resurrection of the body.

THE CREED OF ST RUFINUS OF AQUILAEA
(c. AD 404)

I believe in God, the Father almighty, invisible and impassible, and in Jesus Christ, His only Son, our Lord, who was born of the Virgin Mary by the Holy Spirit, was crucified under Pontius Pilate and was buried. He went down to the dead. On the third day He rose again from the dead. He ascended into heaven, and is seated at the right hand of the Father. From there He shall come to judge the living and the dead. And in the Holy Spirit, the Holy Church, the forgiveness of sins and the resurrection of the body.

THE 'FAITH OF DAMASUS'
(5th century AD)

We believe in one God, the Father almighty, and in our one Lord Jesus Christ, the Son of God, and in [one] Holy Spirit, God. We do not worship and confess three Gods, but one God who is Father and Son and Holy Spirit. He is one God, yet not solitary; He is not at the same time Father to Himself and Son, but the Father is He who begets and the Son He who is begotten. As for the Holy Spirit, He is neither begotten nor unbegotten (ingenious), neither created nor made, but He proceeds from the Father and the Son, being equally eternal and fully equal with the Father and the Son and cooperating with them; for it is written: "By the Word of the Lord the heavens were made," that is, by the Son of God, "and all their host by the breath of His mouth;" and elsewhere: "When you send forth your Spirit, they are created, and you renew the face of the earth." Therefore, in the name of the Father and of the Son and of the Holy Spirit we confess one God, for the term 'God' refers to power, not to personal characteristics. The proper name for the Father is Father, and the proper name for the Son is Son, and the proper name for the Holy Spirit is Holy Spirit. And in this Trinity we believe that God (is) one because what is of one nature and of one substance and of one power with the Father is from one Father. The Father begets the Son, not by an act of will, nor out of necessity, but by nature. In the last times, the Son, who never ceased to be with the Father, came down from the Father to save us and to fulfil the Scriptures. He was conceived from the Holy Spirit and born of the Virgin Mary. He assumed body, soul and sensibility, that is, a complete human nature. He did not lose what He was, but began to be what He was not, in such a way, however, that He is perfect in His own nature and truly shares in ours. For, He who was God has been born as a man, and He who has been born as a man acts as God; and He who acts as God dies as man, and He who dies as man rises again as God. Having conquered the power of death with that body with which He had been born and had suffered and died, He rose again on the third day; He ascended to the Father and is seated at His right hand in the glory which He always has had and always has. We believe that we who have been cleansed in His death and in His blood shall be raised up by Him on the last day in this body in which we now live. It is our hope that we shall receive from Him eternal life, the reward of good merit, or else (we shall receive) the penalty of eternal punishment for sins. Read these words, keep them, subject your soul to this faith. From Christ the Lord you will receive both life and reward.

THE PSEUDO-ATHANASIAN CREED 'QUICUMQUE'
(5th century AD)

Whoever wishes to be saved must, first of all, hold the Catholic faith, for, unless he keeps it whole and inviolate, he will undoubtedly perish for ever. Now this is the Catholic faith: We worship one God in the Trinity and the Trinity in unity, without either confusing the persons or dividing the substance; for the person of the Father is one, the Son's is another, the Holy Spirit's another; but the Godhead of Father, Son and

Holy Spirit is one, their glory equal, their majesty equally eternal. Such as the Father is, such is the Son, such also the Holy Spirit; uncreated is the Father, uncreated the Son, uncreated the Holy Spirit; infinite is the Father, infinite the Son, infinite the Holy Spirit; eternal is the Father, eternal the Son, eternal the Holy Spirit; yet, they are not three eternal beings but one eternal, just as they are not three uncreated beings or three infinite beings but one uncreated and one infinite. In the same way, almighty is the Father, almighty the Son, almighty the Holy Spirit; yet, they are not three almighty beings but one almighty. Thus, the Father is God, the Son is God, the Holy Spirit is God; yet, they are not three gods but one God. Thus, the Father is Lord, the Son is Lord, the Holy Spirit is Lord; yet, they are not three lords but one Lord. For, as the Christian truth compels us to acknowledge each person distinctly as God and Lord, so too the Catholic religion forbids us to speak of three gods or lords. The Father has neither been made by anyone, nor is He created or begotten; the Son is from the Father alone, not made nor created but begotten; the Holy Spirit is from the Father and the Son, not made nor created nor begotten, but proceeding. So there is one Father, not three Fathers; one Son, not three Sons; one Holy Spirit, not three Holy Spirits. And in this Trinity there is no before or after, no greater or lesser, but all three persons are equally eternal with each other and fully equal. Thus, in all things, as has already been stated above, both unity in the Trinity and Trinity in the unity must be worshipped. Let him therefore who wishes to be saved think this of the Trinity. For his eternal salvation it is necessary, however that he should also faithfully believe in the incarnation of our Lord Jesus Christ. Here then is the right faith: We believe and confess that our Lord Jesus Christ, the Son of God, is both and equally God and man. He is God from the substance of the Father, begotten before the ages, and He is man from the substance of a mother, born in time; perfect God and perfect man, composed of a rational soul and a human body; equal to the Father as to His divinity, less than the Father as to His humanity. Although He is God and man, He is nevertheless one Christ, not two; however, not one because the divinity has been changed into a human body, but because the humanity has been assumed into God; entirely one, not by a confusion of substance but by the unity of personhood. For, as a rational soul and a body are a single man, so God and man are one Christ. He suffered for our salvation, went down to the underworld, rose again from the dead on the third day, ascended to the heavens, is seated at the right hand of the Father, wherefrom He shall come to judge the living and the dead. At His coming all men are to rise again with their bodies and to render an account of their own deeds; those who have done good will go to eternal life, but those who have done evil to eternal fire. This is the Catholic faith. Unless one believes it faithfully and firmly, he cannot be saved.

THE CREED OF THE ROMAN ORDER OF BAPTISM
(pre 10th century AD)

I believe in God, the Father almighty, creator of heaven and earth. And in Jesus Christ, His only Son, our Lord, who was conceived by the Holy Spirit, born of the Virgin Mary, suffered under Pontius Pilate, was crucified, died and was buried; He went down to the dead. On the third day He rose again from the dead. He ascended to the heavens, and is seated at the right hand of God, the Father almighty, wherefrom He shall come again to judge the living and the dead. I believe in the Holy Spirit, the Holy Catholic Church, the communion of saints, the forgiveness of sins, the resurrection of the body, and the life everlasting.

CREED OF THE FOURTH LATERAN
GENERAL COUNCIL (AD 1215)

We firmly believe and confess without reservation that there is only one true God, eternal, infinite and unchangeable, incomprehensible, almighty and ineffable, the Father, the Son and the Holy Spirit; three persons indeed but one essence, substance or nature entirely simple. The Father is from no one, the Son from the Father only, and the Holy Spirit equally from both. Without beginning, always and without end, the Father begets, the Son is born and the Holy Spirit proceeds. They are of the same substance and fully equal, equally almighty and equally eternal. (They are) the one principle of the universe, the creator of all things, visible and invisible, spiritual and corporeal, who by His almighty power from the beginning of time made at once out of nothing both orders of creatures, the spiritual and the corporeal, that is, the angelic and the earthly, and then the human creature, who as it were shares in both orders, being composed of spirit and body. For the devil and the other demons were indeed created by God naturally good, but they became evil by their own doing. As for man, he sinned at the suggestion of the devil. This Holy Trinity, undivided according to its common essence and distinct according to the proper characteristics of the persons, communicated the doctrine of salvation to the human race, first through Moses, the holy prophets and its other servants, according to a well ordered disposition of times.

Finally, the only-begotten Son of God, Jesus Christ, whose incarnation is the common work of the whole Trinity, conceived from Mary ever Virgin with the cooperation of the Holy Spirit, made true man, composed of a rational soul and a human body, one person in two natures, showed the way of life more clearly. Though immortal and impassible according to His divinity, He, the very same, became passible and mortal according to His humanity. He also suffered and died on the wood of the cross for the salvation of the human race; He went down to the underworld, rose again from the dead and ascended into heaven; but He went down in the soul, rose again in the body and ascended equally in both. He shall come at the end of time to judge the living and the dead and to render to each one according to his works, to the reprobate as well as to the elect. All of them will rise again with their own bodies which they now bear, to receive according to their works, whether these have been good or evil, the ones perpetual punishment with the devil and the others everlasting glory with Christ.

There is indeed one universal Church of the faithful outside which no one at all is saved, and in which the priest himself, Jesus Christ, is also the sacrifice. His body and blood are truly contained in the sacrament of the altar under the appearances of bread and wine, the bread being transubstantiated into the body by the divine power and the wine into the blood, to the effect that we receive from what is His in what He has received from what is ours in order that the mystery of unity may be accomplished. Indeed, no one can perform this sacrament, except the priest duly ordained according to (the power of) the keys of the Church, which Jesus Christ Himself conceded to the apostles and their successors. The sacrament of baptism (which is celebrated in water at the invocation of God and of the undivided Trinity, viz. the Father, the Son and the Holy Spirit) conduces to the salvation of children as well as of adults when duly conferred by anyone according to the Church's form. If, after receiving baptism, anyone shall have lapsed into sin, he can always be restored through true penance. Not only virgins and the continent, but also married persons, by pleasing God through right faith and good work, merit to attain to eternal happiness.

THE SECOND GENERAL COUNCIL OF LYONS 'PROFESSION OF FAITH OF MICHAEL PALAEOLOGUS' (AD 1274)

First Part

We believe in the Holy Trinity, Father, Son and Holy Spirit, one almighty God; and that in the Trinity the whole Godhead is the same essence, the same substance, equally eternal and equally almighty, of one will, one power and majesty. (This Trinity is) the creator of all things created, from whom, in whom, by whom all things exist in heaven and on earth, the visible and the invisible, the corporeal and the spiritual. We believe that each single person in the Trinity is the one true God, fully and perfectly.

We believe in the Son of God, Word of God, eternally born from the Father, of the same substance, equally almighty and in all things equal to the Father in divinity; born in time, from the Holy Spirit and from Mary ever Virgin, with a rational soul. He has two births, one an eternal birth from the Father, the other a temporal birth from a mother. He is true God and true man, real and perfect in both natures; neither an adoptive son nor an apparent son, but the one and only Son of God, in and from two natures, that is, the divine and the human, in the unity of one person. He is impassible and immortal in His divinity, but in His humanity He suffered for us and for our salvation a true bodily passion; He died, was buried, went down to the dead, and on the third day rose again from the dead by a true bodily resurrection. Forty days after His resurrection He ascended into heaven with His risen body and His soul; He is seated at the right hand of God the Father, wherefrom He shall come to judge the living and the dead and to render to each one according to his works, whether these have been good or evil.

The Apostles' Creed

We believe also in the Holy Spirit, fully, perfectly and truly God, proceeding from the Father and the Son, fully equal, of the same substance, equally almighty and equally eternal with the Father and the Son in all things. We believe that this Holy Trinity is not three gods but one only God, almighty, eternal, invisible and immutable.

We believe that the Holy Catholic and Apostolic Church is the one true Church, in which are given one holy baptism and the true forgiveness of all sins.

We believe also in the true resurrection of this body which we now bear, and in the life eternal. We believe also that God, the Lord almighty, is the one author of the New Testament and the Old, of the Law, the Prophets and the Apostles.

Such is the true Catholic faith, which in the above mentioned articles the most Holy Roman Church holds and preaches.

Second Part

But, because of various errors, introduced by some through ignorance and by others out of malice, she says and preaches: that those who after baptism lapse into sin must not be rebaptized, but obtain pardon for their sins through true penance.

That, if, being truly repentant, they die in charity before having satisfied by worthy fruits of penance for their sins of commission and omission, their souls are cleansed after death by purgatorial and purifying penalties, as Brother John has explained to us; and that to alleviate such penalties the acts of intercession of the living faithful benefit them, namely the sacrifices of the Mass, prayers, alms and other works of piety which the faithful are wont to do for the other faithful according to the Church's institutions.

As for the souls of those who, after having received holy baptism, have incurred no stain of sin whatever, and those souls who, after having contracted the stain of sin, have been cleansed, either while remaining still in their bodies or after having been divested of them as stated above, they are received immediately into heaven.

As for the souls of those who die in mortal sin or with original sin only, they go down immediately to hell, to be punished however with different punishments.

Appendix

The same most Holy Roman Church firmly believes and firmly asserts that nevertheless on the day of Judgment all men will appear with their bodies before the judgment-seat of Christ, to render an account of their own deeds (cf. Rom. 14:10-12).

The same Holy Roman Church also holds and teaches that there are seven sacraments of the Church: one is baptism, which has been mentioned above; another is the sacrament of confirmation which bishops confer by the laying on of hands while they anoint the reborn; then penance, the Eucharist, the sacrament of order, matrimony and extreme unction which, according to the doctrine of the Blessed James, is administered to the sick. The same Roman Church performs the sacrament of the Eucharist with unleavened bread; she holds and teaches that in this sacrament the bread is truly transubstantiated into the body of our Lord Jesus Christ, and the wine into His blood. As regards matrimony, she holds that neither is a man allowed to have several wives at the same time nor a woman several husbands. But, when a legitimate marriage is dissolved by the death of one of the spouses, she declares that a second and afterwards a third wedding are successively licit, if no other canonical impediment goes against it for any reason.

The Holy Roman Church possesses also the highest and full primacy and authority over the universal Catholic Church, which she recognizes in truth and humility to have received with fullness of power from the Lord Himself in the person of Blessed Peter, the chief or head of the apostles, of whom the Roman Pontiff is the successor. And, as she is bound above all to defend the truth of faith, so too, if any questions should arise regarding the faith, they must be decided by her judgment. Anyone accused in matters pertaining to the forum of the Church may appeal to her; and in all causes within the purview of ecclesiastical enquiry, recourse maybe had to her judgment. To her all the Churches are subject; their prelates give obedience and reverence to her. Her fullness of power, moreover, is so firm that she admits the other Churches to a share in her solicitude. The same Roman Church has honored many of those Churches, and chiefly the Patriarchal Churches, with various privileges, its own prerogative being, however, always observed and safeguarded both in general Councils and in some other matters.

THE PROFESSION OF FAITH OF POPE PIUS IV
BULL *INIUNCTUM NOBIS* (AD 1564)

I most firmly accept and embrace the apostolic and ecclesiastical traditions, and all other observances and constitutions of the same Church. I likewise accept Holy Scripture according to that sense which Holy Mother Church has held and does hold, to whom it belongs to judge of the true meaning and interpretation of the Sacred Scriptures; I shall never accept or interpret them otherwise than according to the unanimous consent of the Fathers.

I also profess that there are truly and properly speaking seven sacraments of the New Law, instituted by Jesus Christ our Lord and necessary for the salvation of the human race, though not all are necessary for each individual person: (they are) baptism, confirmation, the Eucharist, penance, extreme unction, order and matrimony. And (I profess) that they confer grace, and that of these, baptism, confirmation and order cannot be repeated without sacrilege. I also admit and accept the rites received and approved in the Catholic Church for the administration of all the sacraments mentioned above.

I embrace and accept each and all the articles defined and declared by the most Holy Synod of Trent concerning original sin and justification.

I also profess that in the Mass there is offered to God a true sacrifice, properly speaking, which is propitiatory for the living and the dead, and that in the most Holy Sacrament of the Eucharist the body and blood together with the soul and the divinity of our Lord Jesus Christ are truly, really and substantially present, and that there takes place a change (*conversio*) of the whole substance of bread into the body and of the whole substance of wine into the blood; and this change the Catholic Church calls transubstantiation. I also confess that under each species alone (*sub altera tantum specie*) the whole and entire Christ and the true sacrament is received.

I steadfastly hold that there is a purgatory, and that the souls detained there are helped by the acts of intercession (*suffragiis*) of the faithful; likewise, that the saints reigning together with Christ should be venerated and invoked, that they offer prayers to God for us, and that their relics should be venerated. I firmly declare that the images of Christ and of the Mother of God ever Virgin and of the other saints as well are to be kept and preserved, and that due honour and veneration should be given to them. I also affirm that the power of indulgences has been left by Christ to the Church, and that their use is very beneficial to the Christian people.

I acknowledge the Holy, Catholic and Apostolic, Roman Church as the mother and the teacher of all the Churches, and I promise and swear true obedience to the Roman Pontiff, successor of Blessed Peter, chief of the apostles, and Vicar of Christ.

I unhesitantly accept and profess also all other things transmitted, defined and declared by the sacred canons and the ecumenical Councils, especially by the most Holy Council of Trent [and by the ecumenical Vatican Council, mostly as regards the primacy of the Roman Pontiff and his infallible teaching authority].[1] At the same time, all contrary propositions and whatever heresies have been condemned, rejected and anathematized by the Church, I too condemn, reject and anathematize.

This true Catholic faith, outside of which no one can be saved, which of my own accord I now profess and truly hold, I, N.,_____ do promise, vow and swear that, with the help of God, I shall most faithfully keep and confess entire and inviolate, to my last breath, and that I shall take care, as far as it lies in my power, that it be held, taught and preached by those under me, or those over whom I have charge by virtue of my office. So help me God and these His Holy Gospels.

THE PROFESSION OF FAITH OF POPE PAUL VI
CREDO OF THE PEOPLE OF GOD
(AD 1968)

We believe in one God, Father, Son and Holy Spirit, creator of things visible - such as this world in which our brief life runs its course - and of things invisible-such as the pure spirits which are also called angels - and creator in each man of his spiritual and immortal soul.

We believe that this only God is as absolutely one in His infinitely Holy essence as in His other perfections: in His almighty power,

---

[1] [Additional words inserted in the creed under Pope Pius IX].

His infinite knowledge, His providence, His will and His love. He is 'He who is' as He revealed to Moses (cf. Ex. 3:14 Vulg.); He is 'Love', as the apostle John has taught us (cf. 1 Jn 4:8); so that these two names, Being and Love, express ineffably the same divine essence of Him who has wished to make Himself manifest to us, and who, "dwelling in unapproachable light" (1 Tim. 6:16), is in Himself above every name and every created thing and every created intellect. God alone can give us right and full knowledge of Himself, by revealing Himself as Father, Son and Holy Spirit, in whose eternal life we are by grace called to share, here on earth in the obscurity of faith and after death in eternal light. The mutual bonds which from all eternity constitute the three persons, each of whom is one and the same divine Being, constitute the blessed inmost life of the most Holy God, infinitely beyond all that we can humanly understand. We give thanks, however, to the divine goodness that very many believers can testify with us before men to the unity of God, even though they know not the mystery of the most Holy Trinity.

We believe then in God who eternally begets the Son; we believe in the Son, the Word of God, who is eternally begotten; we believe in the Holy Spirit, the uncreated person who proceeds from the Father and the Son as their eternal love. Thus, in the three divine persons who are "equally eternal and fully equal" the life and beatitude of God, perfectly one, superabound and are consummated in the supreme excellence and glory proper to the uncreated essence, and always "both unity in the Trinity and Trinity in the unity must be worshipped."

We believe in our Lord Jesus Christ, the Son of God. He is the eternal Word, born of the Father before all ages and of one same substance with the Father, that is consubstantial (*homo-ousios*) with the Father; through Him all things were made. He became flesh from the Virgin Mary by the Holy Spirit and was made man. Therefore, He is "equal to the Father as to His divinity, less than the Father as to His humanity", entirely one "not by a confusion of substance" (which is impossible), "but by the unity of personhood."

He dwelled among us, full of grace and truth. He proclaimed and established the Kingdom of God, making the Father manifest to us. He gave us His new commandment to love one another as He Himself loved us. He taught us the way of the beatitudes of the Gospel: poverty in spirit, meekness, suffering borne with patience, thirst after justice, mercy, purity of heart, peace-making, persecution suffered for justice sake. He suffered under Pontius Pilate, He, the Lamb of God bearing the sins of the world; He died for us, nailed to the cross, saving us by His redeeming blood. He was buried and, of His own power, rose again on the third day, raising us by His resurrection to that sharing in the divine life which is the life of grace. He ascended into heaven, wherefrom He shall come again, this time in glory, to judge the living and the dead, each according to his merits: those who have responded to the love and goodness of God will go to eternal life, but those who have rejected them to the end will be sentenced to the fire that will never be extinguished. And to His Kingdom there will be no end.

We believe in the Holy Spirit, the Lord and Giver of life, who together with the Father and the Son is worshipped and glorified. He has spoken through the prophets; He was sent to us by Christ after His resurrection and His ascension to the Father; He enlightens, vivifies, protects and guides the Church; He purifies her members if they do not refuse His grace. His action, which penetrates to the inmost of the soul, enables man to respond to the command of Jesus: "You must be perfect as your heavenly Father is perfect" (Mt. 5:48).

We believe that Mary, who remained ever a Virgin, is the Mother of the Incarnate Word, our God and Savior Jesus Christ, and that, by reason of her singular election, "she was, in consideration of the merits of her Son, redeemed in a more eminent manner" (LG 53)[2], "preserved immune from all stain of original sin", and "by an exceptional gift of grace stands far above all other creatures" (LG 53).

Joined by a close and indissoluble bond to the mysteries of the incarnation and redemption (cf. LG 53, 58, 61), the Blessed Virgin Mary, the Immaculate, "when the course of her earthly life was finished, was taken up, body and soul, to the glory of heaven" and, likened to her Son who rose again from the dead, she received in anticipation the future lot of all the just. We believe that the Holy Mother of God, the new Eve, "Mother of the Church" (LG 53, 56, 61), "continues in heaven to exercise her maternal role" with regard to Christ's members, "helping to bring forth and to increase the divine life in the souls of all the redeemed" (LG 62).

---

[2] *Lumen Gentium*, Vatican Council II, Dogmatic Constitution on the Church, 1964.

The Apostles' Creed

We believe that in Adam all have sinned, which means that the original offense committed by him caused the human race, common to all, to fall to a state in which it bears the consequences of that offense. This is no longer the state in which the human nature was at the beginning in our first parents, constituted as they were in holiness and justice, and in which man was immune from evil and death. And so, it is human nature so fallen, deprived from the gift of grace with which it had first been adorned, injured in its own natural powers and subjected to the dominion of death, that is communicated to all men; it is in this sense that every man is born in sin. We therefore hold, with the Council of Trent, that original sin is transmitted with human nature "by propagation, not by imitation" and that it "is in all men, proper to each."

We believe that our Lord Jesus Christ by the sacrifice of the Cross redeemed us from original sin and all the personal sins committed by each one of us, so that the word of the apostle is verified: "Where sin increased, grace abounded all the more" (Rom. 5:20).

We believe in and confess one baptism instituted by our Lord Jesus Christ for the forgiveness of sins. Baptism should be administered even to little children "who of themselves cannot have yet committed any sin," in order that, though born deprived of supernatural grace, they may be reborn "of water and the Holy Spirit" to the divine life in Christ Jesus.

We believe in one, Holy, Catholic and apostolic Church, built by Jesus Christ on that rock which is Peter. She is the "Mystical Body of Christ," at once a visible society "provided with hierarchical organs" and a "spiritual community; the Church on earth," the pilgrim People of God here below, and "the Church filled with heavenly blessings"; "the germ and the first fruits of the Kingdom of God", through which the work and the sufferings of redemption are continued throughout human history, and which looks with all its strength for the perfect accomplishment it will obtain beyond time in glory (LG 8, 5). In the course of time, the Lord Jesus Christ forms His Church by means of the sacraments emanating from His fullness (LG 7, 11). For, by these the Church makes her members share in the mystery of the death and resurrection of Jesus Christ, through the grace of the Holy Spirit who gives her life and movement (SC 5, 6; LG 7,12,50). She is therefore holy, though having sinners in her midst, because she herself has no other life but the life of grace. If they live by her life, her members are sanctified; if they move away from her life, they fall into sins and disorders that prevent the radiation of her sanctity. This is why she suffers and does penance for those offenses, of which she has the power to free her children through the blood of Christ and the gift of the Holy Spirit.

Heiress of the divine promise and daughter of Abraham according to the Spirit, through that Israel whose sacred Scriptures she lovingly guards, and whose patriarchs and prophets she venerates; founded upon the apostles and faithfully handing down through the centuries their ever-living word and their powers as pastors in the successor of Peter and the bishops in communion with him; perpetually assisted by the Holy Spirit, the Church has the charge of guarding, teaching, explaining and spreading the truth which God revealed dimly to men through the prophets, and then fully in the Lord Jesus. We believe all "that is contained in the word of God, written or handed down, and that the Church proposes for belief as divinely revealed, whether by a solemn decree or by the ordinary and universal teaching office." We believe in the infallibility enjoyed by the successor of Peter when, as pastor and teacher of all the Christians, "he speaks ex cathedra" and which "also resides in the episcopal Body when it exercises with him the supreme teaching office" (LG 25).

We believe that the Church founded by Jesus Christ and for which He prayed is indefectibly one in faith, worship and the bond of hierarchical communion (LG 8, 18-23; UR 2). In the bosom of this Church, the rich variety of liturgical rites and the legitimate diversity of theological and spiritual heritages and of special disciplines, far from "injuring her unity, make it more manifest" (LG 23; OE 2-6).

Recognizing also the existence, "outside the organism" of the Church of Christ of "numerous elements of sanctification and truth which, because they belong to her as her own, call for Catholic unity" (LG 8), and believing in the action of the Holy Spirit who stirs up in the heart of all the disciples of Christ a desire for this unity (LG 15), we entertain the hope that the Christians who do not yet enjoy full communion in one only Church will at last be united in one flock with only one Shepherd.

We believe that "the Church is necessary for salvation. For, Christ, who is the sole Mediator and the one way to salvation, makes

Himself present for us in His Body which is the Church" (LG 14). But the divine design of salvation embraces all men; and those "who without fault on their part do not know the Gospel of Christ and His Church but seek God with a sincere heart, and under the influence of grace endeavor to do His will as recognized through the prompting of their conscience", they too in a number known only to God "can obtain eternal salvation" (LG 16).

We believe that the Mass, celebrated by the priest representing the person of Christ by virtue of the power received through the sacrament of Order, and offered by him in the name of Christ and of the members of His Mystical Body, is indeed the sacrifice of Calvary rendered sacramentally present on our altars. We believe that, as the bread and wine consecrated by the Lord at the Last Supper were changed into His body and His blood which were soon to be offered for us on the Cross, likewise the bread and wine consecrated by the priest are changed into the body and blood of Christ enthroned gloriously in heaven; and we believe that the mysterious presence of the Lord, under the species which continue to appear to our senses as before, is a true, real and substantial presence.

Thus, in this sacrament Christ cannot become present otherwise than by the change of the whole substance of bread into His body, and the change of the whole substance of wine into His blood, while only the properties of the bread and wine which our senses perceive remain unchanged. This mysterious change is fittingly and properly named by the Church transubstantiation. Every theological explanation which seeks some understanding of this mystery must, in order to be in accord with Catholic faith, maintain firmly that in the order of reality itself, independently of our mind, the bread and wine have ceased to exist after the consecration, so that it is the adorable body and blood of the Lord Jesus which from then on are really before us under the sacramental species of bread and wine, as the Lord willed it, in order to give Himself to us as food and to bind us together in the unity of His Mystical Body.

The unique and indivisible existence of the Lord glorious in heaven is not multiplied, but is rendered present by the sacrament in the many places on earth where the eucharistic sacrifice is celebrated. And this existence remains present, after the celebration of the sacrifice, in the Blessed Sacrament which is in the tabernacle as the living heart of our churches. Therefore, it is our sweet duty to honor and adore, in the Blessed Host which our eyes see, the Incarnate Word Himself whom they cannot see and who, yet, without leaving heaven, is made present before us.

We confess also that the Kingdom of God, begun here on earth in the Church of Christ, is not "of this world" (Jn 18:36) whose "form is passing away" (1 Cor. 7:31), and that its proper growth cannot be identified with the progress of civilization, of science or of human technology, but that it consists in an ever more profound knowledge of the unfathomable riches of Christ, an ever stronger hope of eternal blessings, an ever more ardent response to the love of God, and finally in an ever more abundant diffusion of grace and holiness among men. But it is this same love which impels the Church to be also continuously concerned about the true temporal welfare of men. While she never ceases to remind all her children that "they have not" here on earth "a lasting city" (Heb. 13:14), she also urges them to contribute, each according to his condition of life and his means, to the welfare of their earthly city, to promote justice, peace and fraternal concord among men, to give their help generously to their brothers, especially to the poorest and most unfortunate. The deep solicitude of the Church, the Spouse of Christ, for the needs of men, for their joys and hopes, their griefs and efforts, is therefore nothing other than the desire which strongly urges her to be present to them in order to enlighten them with the light of Christ and to gather and unite them all in Him, their only Savior. This solicitude can never be understood to mean that the Church conforms herself to the things of this world or that the ardor is lessened with which she expects her Lord and the eternal Kingdom.

We believe in the life eternal. We believe that the souls of all those who die in the grace of Christ - whether they must still be purified in purgatory, or, from the moment they leave their bodies, Jesus takes them to paradise as He did for the good thief - constitute the People of God beyond death; death will be finally vanquished on the day of the resurrection when these souls will be re-united with their bodies.

We believe that the multitude of those gathered around Jesus and Mary in paradise forms the Church of heaven where in the enjoyment of eternal beatitude they see God as He is (1 Jn 3:2), and where they also, in different ways and degrees, are associated with the holy angels in the divine rule exercised by the glorified Christ, by interceding for us and by providing with their brotherly solicitude a powerful help to our infirmity (LG 49).

We believe in the communion of all the faithful of Christ, those who are pilgrims on earth, the dead who are being purified, and the blessed in heaven, all together forming one Church; and we also believe that in this communion the merciful love of God and His saints is ever turning listening ears to our prayers, as Jesus told us: "Ask and you will receive" (Jn 16:24). Confessing this faith and sustained by this hope, we look forward to the resurrection of the dead and the life of the world to come. Blessed be God thrice Holy, Amen.

POPE JOHN PAUL II
CONGREGATION FOR THE
DOCTRINE OF THE FAITH
NEW FORMULA FOR THE PROFESSION OF FAITH
(25th February 1989)

The formula of the profession of faith repeats in its entirety the first part of the text in effect since 1967 which contains the Nicene-Constantinopolitan Creed. The second part has been modified and subdivided into three paragraphs so as to distinguish better the type of truth and the corresponding assent that is sought.

Profession of Faith

I, N._____, with firm faith believe and profess each and every thing (*omnia et singula*) that is contained in the symbol of faith, namely, [There follows the text of the Symbol of Nicaea-Constantinople as used in the Mass of the Roman Rite].

With firm faith I believe as well everything (*ea omnia*) contained in God's word, written or handed down in tradition and proposed by the Church—whether in solemn judgment or in the ordinary and universal Magisterium—as divinely revealed and requiring to be believed (*tamquam divinitus revelata credenda*).

I also firmly accept and hold each and every thing (*omnia et singula*) that is proposed by that same Church definitively (*definitive*) with regard to teaching concerning faith and morals. What is more, I adhere (*adhaereo*) with religious submission of will and intellect (*religioso voluntatis et intellectus obsequio*) to the teachings which either the Roman pontiff or the college of bishops enunciate when they exercise the authentic magisterium even if they proclaim those teachings in an act that is not definitive.

About the Author

Robert M. Haddad holds qualifications in law, theology, philosophy and religious education, namely, a LL.B (USyd.), Grad. Cert. in RE (Charles Sturt Uni.), Grad. Dip. Ed. (ACU), Grad. Dip. in Teacher Ed. (College of Teachers, London), AMLP (Oxon.), MA Theo. Studies (UNDA – University Medalist), MRelEd (UNDA) and a M. Phil (ACU). For his M. Phil. Robert researched the apologetical arguments of St Justin Martyr.

In addition to his studies, Robert has also authored various books, including *Lord of History Series* (2 volumes), *Law and Life*, *The Family and Human Life*, *Defend the Faith!*, *The Case for Christianity – St Justin Martyr's Arguments for Religious Liberty and Judicial Justice*, *Answering the Anti-Catholic Challenge* (ch. 3) and *1001 Reasons Why it's Great to be Catholic!*

From 1990-2005, Robert worked full-time at St Charbel's College, Sydney, teaching Religion and History. He held the positions of Year Co-ordinator and Religious Education Co-ordinator concurrently for ten years and was Assistant Principal (Welfare) for six years.

From 2006-2008, Robert worked full-time as the Convener of the Catholic Chaplaincy at the University of Sydney. He was also a lecturer at the Center for Thomistic Studies for eleven years (1996-2008), teaching Apologetics, Church Fathers and Church History, as well as assisting part-time with *Lumen Verum Apologetics* (1996-present) and the Catholic Adult Education Centre (2010-2013).

From 2009-2012, Robert was the Director of the Confraternity of Christian Doctrine (Sydney) and in that capacity was the chief editor of the revised *Christ our Light and Life* (3rd Edition) religious education K-12 curriculum used by Catholic students in state schools as well as the *Gratia Series* sacramental programs for children preparing for Reconciliation, First Holy Communion, and Confirmation in the Archdiocese of Sydney. He has recently also edited a new RCIA resource for use in Catholic schools in the same Archdiocese entitled *Initiate*.

In 2014, Robert was awarded an Australia Day Award by the Australia Day Council of New South Wales for his overall contribution to education. Currently, he is the Head of New Evangelization for the Catholic Education Office (Sydney) and lectures/tutors in Theology at the University of Notre Dame, Sydney. From time to time Robert also appears on the Telepace Television Network and Voice of Charity radio.

Other Works by the Author

Introduction to the Greatest Fathers of the Church (Parousia Media, 1999)

A Seat at the Supper (General Editor; author Frank Colyer, self-published, 2001)

Introduction to Early Church History (Parousia Media, 2002)

Law and Life (Parousia Media, 2004)

The Case for Christianity – St Justin Martyr's Arguments for Religious Liberty and Judicial Justice (Connor Court Publishing, 2009)

The Family and Human Life (2nd Ed. co-authored with Bernard Toutounji, Parousia Media, 2011)

Defend the Faith! (Parousia Media, 2012)

Answering the Anti-Catholic Challenge (General Editor and author of ch. 3, Modotti Press, 2012)

1001 Reasons Why it's Great to be Catholic! (Parousia Media, 2014)

Christ our Light and Life (General Editor 3rd Edition, 2012) religious education curriculum K-12 used by Catholic students in government schools throughout the state of New South Wales.

Gratia Series (General Editor, 2012) sacramental programs for children preparing for Reconciliation, First Holy Communion, and Confirmation in the Archdiocese of Sydney.

Initiate (General Editor, CEO Sydney Publications, 2014), a RCIA resource for use in Catholic schools in the Archdiocese of Sydney.

www.ingramcontent.com/pod-product-compliance
Lightning Source LLC
Chambersburg PA
CBHW071525080526
44588CB00011B/1562